Simple and Practical

Accounting with Computers

Simple and Practical

Accounting with Computers

A Guide to the Benefits of Computerised Accounts

Keith Kirkland and Stuart Howard

**KOGAN
PAGE**

First published in 1998

Kogan Page Limited
120 Pentonville Road
London N1 9JN

© Vector Business Development, 1998

Illustrations by John Loader

British Library Cataloguing in Publication Data

A CIP record for this book is available from the British Library

ISBN 0 7494 2942 9

Typeset by Vector Business Development.
Printed and bound in Great Britain by Bell & Bain Ltd, Glasgow.

Contents

Benefits of Computerised Accounting

Thousands of businesses, large and small, have benefited by installing a computerised accounting system.

We cannot promise that computers will help you give up smoking, stop your socks smelling or make you more attractive to the opposite sex. We do, however, feel that we ought to start this book with a summary of the benefits which computerisation can bring to your business.

Help With Book-keeping

Most businesses start out in a small way. To begin with their book-keeping may be restricted to recording 'cash in' and 'cash out' in an analysed cashbook. As the business grows, more details are needed so the cash book grows. Eventually you need a cash book a metre wide, and you still wouldn't be able to record all of the details required!

Your cashbook grows!

1

In the old days, a business may have moved to a manual double entry system, but this makes no sense today. Manual double entry takes too much time to learn, practise and use. Your manual book-keeping records cannot produce management reports automatically like the computer can. The only practical accounting system beyond the cash book is computerised accounting. Despite the silly assertion to the contrary, mistakes are hardly ever the computer's fault. If the computer makes a mistake, it is usually because a human gave it the wrong information to start with!

If your manual bookkeeping system is running out of steam, you should consider computerised accounting.

Help With Sales Administration

If you sell goods or services on credit, you will already know that this involves a great deal of administration.

Here are some ways in which a computerised accounting system can help you:

- improve the neatness and accuracy of your invoices
- track credit limits so customers can't exceed the limit that you have set them
- calculate trade discounts accurately
- calculate VAT accurately
- generate customer statements with little effort
- print remittance advices
- give you an aged debt list (this will tell you who owes money and for how long)
- generate personalised debt chasing letters.

If you have problems invoicing customers or collecting debts, you will benefit from computerised accounting.

Help With Wages Calculations

Manual payroll calculations can be a nightmare. Using tax and national insurance tables for even a small number of employees is very time consuming. Here are some of the areas when the computer will help:

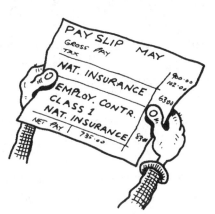

- calculating gross pay
- calculating amounts owed to the Inland Revenue
- calculating amounts owed to the Department of Social Security
- writing payslips
- entering the wages deductions into the accounts
- administering Statutory Sick Pay
- administering Statutory Maternity Pay
- producing year-end returns, etc.

A computerised payroll can be a real time-saver. Not only will it generate payslips automatically, it will also produce your year-end tax returns as well. For employees who are paid the same amount each period, you don't even need to update the amount – just run the payroll!

Payroll programs help you cope with exceptional items. For example, you have to be aware of special treatments for directors' national insurance, expenses and benefits in kind, pensions etc. The payroll program will remember all these details and calculate wages and salaries accordingly.

The output from the payroll program can be connected to a bankers electronic payment system. This way, the wages calculated by the program are transmitted to the employees' bank accounts automatically.

If you employ more than half a dozen people, you should consider a computerised payroll program.

Help With Purchasing Administration

If you buy a lot of goods or services on credit, you could benefit from the installation of a computerised purchase ledger.

Your purchase ledger keeps track of how much you owe suppliers who provide you with goods or services on credit. You can use the purchase ledger to help plan your expenditure. On the one hand, you don't want to pay too quickly. On the other hand, you don't want to pay so slowly that your suppliers put you on their 'stop' list. Your purchase ledger program will help you decide who, and when, to pay.

In many businesses, purchased items are charged to individual jobs or departments. Your computer program can allocate purchased items to these areas quickly and easily.

If you have large numbers of items bought on credit, you should consider a computerised accounting system.

Dealing With the Bank

You probably won't see your bank manager very often if your account is in credit. However, if you need a loan or overdraft, you may need to convince the bank manager (or lending manager) that your business is in a position to meet the repayments. Evidence for this may be provided in the form of accounts for past years together with cash (or profit) projections for the future.

Your computer will produce management reports which you can use to convince the bank that you are credit worthy.

Better Quality Information for Your Accountant

The computer can produce the sort of information that many businesses once went to their accountant for. Provided the quality of your book-keeping is good, your accountant won't be shedding any tears. This is because you are no longer asking him to do the donkey work.

Good computerised accounting records will enable your accountant/auditor to produce your annual accounts quickly and economically. You may also find that your accountant's bills are reduced. This is because much of your accountant's cost may be incurred checking your manual book-keeping records. Your accountant may be spending time completing your book-keeping entries for you. You will save your accountant's time and cost to yourself if you enter book-keeping information conscientiously into a computerised accounting program.

Most accounts software will produce a draft profit and loss account and balance sheet for the accountant to start work on. This can be a real time saver. It is unlikely that the 'raw' accounts produced by your accounting program will show a 'perfect' profit figure. This is because a 'proper' set of accounts includes a lot of accounting adjustments which may not be incorporated in the raw accounts produced by your computer. These adjustments include accruals, prepayments, depreciation, tax allowable versus non tax allowable expenditure etc. You will still need an accountant to adjust the accounts for you. However, even if the computer produces accounts which need adjustments, you will still have saved a great deal of time, effort and money along the way.

If you want to reduce your accountant's bills, you should consider computerised accounting.

Better Quality Information for the Taxman

You may not regard the idea of supplying the tax man with clear information as a benefit. However, in our experience, clearly presented tax information can save a great deal of time in form filling and answering follow-up questions.

The Inland Revenue will appreciate accurate and prompt returns. Failing to file your returns on time can attract penalties. HM Customs and Excise also demand prompt returns. They can levy fines for late returns and late payments.

If your business turnover is below the VAT registration threshold, you don't have to account for VAT at all. However, once your turnover exceeds the VAT registration limit, you have to register for VAT and submit returns to Customs and Excise. Of course, you can account for VAT using a cashbook – especially if you are on the cash accounting scheme. Even so, VAT is more easily calculated in a computerised accounting package.

When your sales turnover exceeds the cash accounting limit, you have to account for VAT using the 'tax point' date. Tax point accounting for VAT is a nightmare which involves a great deal of administration. Computerised accounting for VAT is virtually essential if you are a tax point trader.

Computers produce the VAT return figures at the press of a button. You can also ask for a list of the book-keeping entries which made up that VAT return. This is useful if the VAT man asks questions. Some packages even print out a copy of the VAT return for you. This makes VAT administration as painless as possible.

A change in VAT status from non registered to registered, or from cash accounting to tax point accounting, could be the trigger point for you to change over to computerised accounting.

Better Quality Information for You

We have saved the most important benefit till last.

With manual systems, most businesses find it hard to make time for even the basic book-keeping entries. There is little time left over to decipher what those entries mean in terms of business performance. However, once information has been entered into a computer, it can be analysed automatically by the program to give meaningful reports. At the very least, you need answers to the following questions:

- How much money have I got?
- Where does my money come from?
- Where does my money go to?
- How much do I owe others?
- How much do they owe me?
- Am I trading profitably?

Unless you can answer these basic questions, you are not in control of the business.

Of course, you don't have to stop there. Once you can answer the basic questions, you can develop the financial reporting as far as you want. Most computerised accounting programs have reports pre-programmed into them. Here are some typical examples.

- top customer list
- bank receipts and payments
- aged debt reports
- customer trading history
- VAT report details
- profit and loss account
- balance sheet
- departmental budgets
- expense account history
- fixed asset list, etc.

With the computer, it is possible to generate management reports which previously were the provenance of much larger companies.

You may even be able to 'export' information from your accounts package to your word processor, spreadsheet or database package which will enable you to enhance the appearance of the information still further.

If you need to improve your financial reporting, you should consider computerised accounting.

Summary

There are many areas where computerised accounting brings benefits. The effort of installing a computerised accounting system will be repaid many times over.

Once you have taken the plunge and computerised, you will be able to harness the computer's power to manipulate and present information. This puts you in control of the business so that it works for you rather than the other way round. However, there are many problems and pitfalls which lie in wait for anybody trying to computerise their manual accounting system. If the following chapters sound like a catalogue of disasters, remember that thousands of small businesses have installed computerised accounting systems successfully. Most of these businesses wonder how they ever managed without it.

We are not saying that everything is plain sailing; the *transition* between manual and computerised accounts can be particularly traumatic. However, if the problems listed in this chapter are familiar to you, computerised accounting could deliver real benefits. With benefits like these, can you really afford to ignore computerised accounting?

Chapter 2

Types of Accounts Packages

A computerised accounts package comprises a 'family' of accounting programs which run on a computer. For the size of business we are considering in this book, the computer will almost certainly be an IBM compatible personal computer.

There are many types of packages on offer. In order to give you some idea of the range, we have classified them into the following five broad categories:

- Financial Organisers.
- Integrated Packages.
- Junior Packages.
- Full Blown Module Packages.
- Industry Specific Packages.

Here is an explanation of each.

Financial Organisers

These packages are designed to help individuals and very small businesses control their bank accounts. They are cash based. They cannot cope with accounting for debtors and creditors.

They help you reconcile the bank account. They also produce reports and graphs which help you understand your finances.

Some can track a share portfolio, produce an asset register for insurance purposes or help with VAT. One even offers an interface with an invoicing package, reminiscent of the modular approach of the larger packages.

Examples:

- *Quicken* from Intuit
- *Money* from Microsoft
- *Moneywise* from Sage.

Price guide:

- Around £50 (although they can often be had for less).

We will not be spending further time on these packages. Although they are excellent products in their own right, they do not have the business emphasis which we need.

Integrated Packages

These packages are not based on separate programs (or 'modules' as they are often called). They comprise a complete self-contained, integrated package which covers most financial aspects. Previously, you had to buy separate programs for each accounting task.

These are comparative newcomers to the accounting package scene. Whereas their predecessors tended to mimic manual systems on the computer, integrated packages really flex the computer's ability to solve the book-keeping problem.

They offer a great deal of flexibility enabling you to make changes at almost any time. You can also access any part of the system so there are very few restrictions on the way you work.

With an integrated package, you could be more restricted by the capacity of your computer's disk and memory space than by the program itself.

Examples:

- *Quickbooks* from Intuit
- *TAS Books* from Megatech Software
- *Instant Accounting*' from Sage.

Price guide:

- Around £100 although you should watch for special offers.

'Junior' Packages

The longer established accounting software companies like Sage and Pegasus became involved in computer software in the late seventies and early eighties. They either:

- developed an accounting package for small business using PCs (and later developed a larger, more comprehensive version for mainframes), or

- they already had a full scale mainframe package which they 'cut down' for use by the smaller business.

These packages tend to talk about nominal ledgers, sales ledgers etc and stress their book-keeping origins rather more proudly than their integrated competitors. However, the two types of packages are rapidly becoming indistinguishable as the integrated packages become more comprehensive and the 'junior' packages become more user-friendly.

Examples:

- *Solo* from Pegasus
- *Sage Line 50* from Sage.

Price Guide

- £200–£700 depending on the features offered. Some of the lower end products have dropped in price to compete with integrated packages.

Full Blown, Modular Packages

These systems cope with the demands of large organisations requiring sophisticated accounting solutions. The complete system is quite expensive but it will handle large amounts of data and more complex accounting requirements. We anticipate that most people reading this book will not need this type of system – yet!

Examples:

- *Opera* from Pegasus
- *Sage Line 100* from Sage
- *SunSystems* from Systems Union.

Price Guide:

- Expect to spend at least £1,000 possibly £1,500 per module or more – serious money.

Industry Specific Packages

Businesses in the same industry tend to have similar accounting needs. This has prompted software suppliers to write packages for specific industries like the insurance industry, hotel, motor trades and builders. The software writers claim that 'sector specific' packages fit the business requirements more closely than a general package. In many instances, they do. However, if you are thinking of buying one of these packages, check whether the software house has a big enough customer base to make it financially worthwhile for them to continue supporting the package. How would you feel if you were totally dependent on one industry-specific accounting package and the package developed problems after the software house stopped trading?

In the next chapter, we will look at a typical integrated accounts package called *Instant Accounting*. This is a typical introductory package for small and medium sized businesses.

Chapter 3

A Typical Package –
Sage Instant Accounting

Inside the back cover of this book, you will find a trial copy of *Sage Instant Accounting*. We will use this package to illustrate the points in this book. If you have access to a personal computer, we suggest you install *Instant Accounting* and refer to the screens on the PC as you work through this text.

How to Install *Instant Accounting* on Windows 95

- Insert your 'Instant' CD into your CD-ROM drive.

- Open the 'Start' menu and choose the 'Run' option. The Run dialogue box appears.

- In the 'Open' box, type **D:\setup** then choose the 'OK' button. (If you are installing from a different drive, replace D: in the above command with the appropriate drive letter.)

- Follow the on-screen instructions to complete the installation.

How to Install Instant Accounting on Windows 3.11

- Insert your 'Instant' CD into your CD-ROM drive.

- Open the 'File' menu from the Program Manager menu bar and choose the 'Run' option. The Run dialogue box appears.

- In the Command Line text box, type **D:\setup** then choose the OK button. (If you are installing from a different drive, replace D: in the above command with the appropriate drive letter.)

- Follow the on-screen instructions to complete the installation.

We recommend that you accept the default values offered by the program during installation.

Once the program is installed, you will be presented with the following screen.

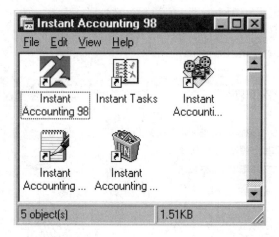

We suggest that you run the *Instant Accounting Tour* by double clicking the Instant Tour icon.

When you have completed the tour, you can load the *Instant Accounting* program either by:

- double clicking the desktop icon, or
Instant
Accounting 98

- from the Start menu by selecting 'Start' followed by 'Programs' followed by 'Instant Accounting 98' as follows.

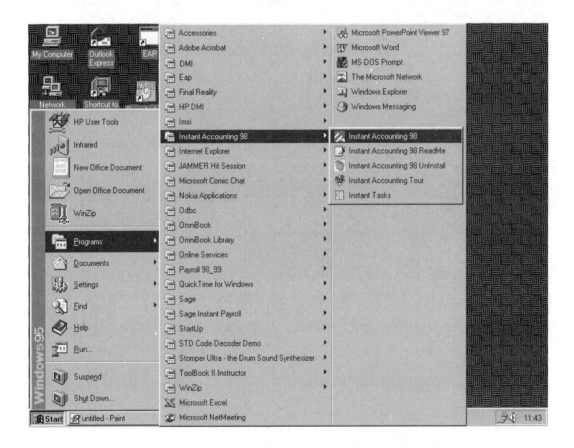

After a short while, the program will load and you will be presented with the following screen.

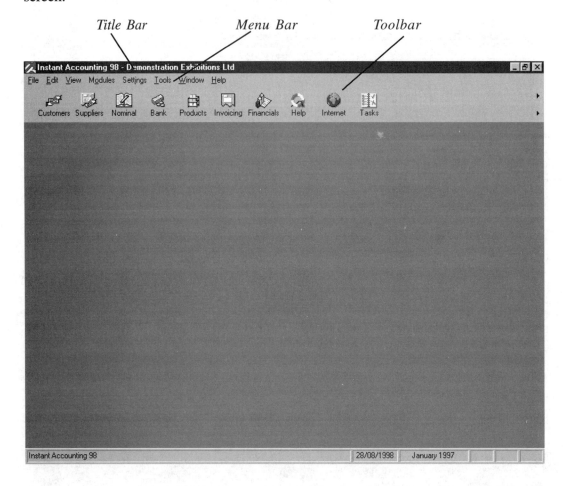

At the top of the screen, you can see three horizontal bands of information. These are:

Title Bar – the top line gives the program name (ie *Instant Accounting 98)* and the name of the business, eg Demonstration Exhibitions Ltd.

Menu Bar – the next line of information is called the menu bar. This contains menus for File, Edit, View, Modules, Settings etc. We recommend that you use the menu bar to load demonstration data for Demonstration Exhibitions Ltd as follows. Click on 'File', this will bring up the following menu.

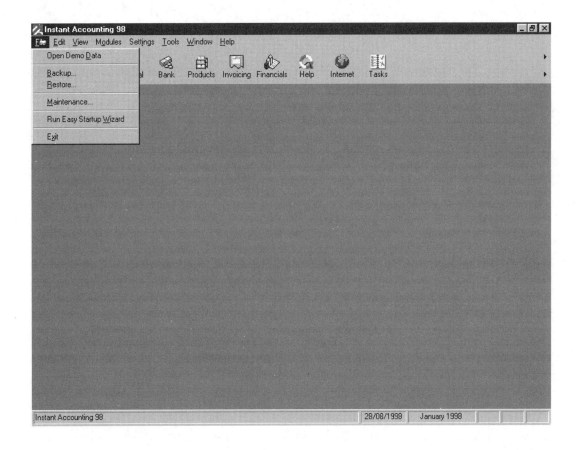

The top option in the menu box will be either 'Open Instant Data' or 'Open Demo Data'. Click the top option (if necessary) to make it read 'Open Demo Data'.

Toolbar – Below the menu bar is the toolbar. The toolbar contains a series of small pictures in boxes. These pictures are more properly called icons. Each icon has a word below it describing the purpose of that icon. We will shortly use the icons to navigate around the program.

This is what each icon does.

The 'Customers' option enables you to set up customer accounts, raise invoices, issue statements and control debt using aged debt reports. This ledger is particularly valuable to businesses operating credit sales.

The 'Suppliers' option enables you to set up supplier accounts and record invoices billed to you. It also enables you to check how much business you are doing with each supplier and manage your cash outflows for supplier payments.

The 'Nominal' option is used to record amounts of money passing through the accounts. It records receipts from sales, loans in and overdraft etc. It records expenditure on items like wages, expenses, capital equipment, stock, subcontractor payments etc.

This option records money movements. Money can be channelled through three avenues. These are banks, cash and credit cards. You can, of course, transfer money between accounts. You can use this option to reconcile the bank account with your own accounting records.

This option is particularly useful to businesses which sell goods. Each type of product is given a product code, product description, selling price, VAT code and unit of sale. Storing product details in this way saves a huge amount of time. When you raise invoices, you only have to call up the product code and all of the detail is entered onto the invoice automatically without the need for further typing.

Raising sales invoices can take a lot of time. It is easy to make mistakes with items like the price, discount, delivery address, VAT rate etc. The invoicing option simplifies raising of invoices and delivers a level of neatness which is difficult to match by manual typing. Invoices raised by the system can be posted automatically to the accounts. This means that your records are always up to date, leaving you in complete control of the sales side of the business.

This option helps you to control your finances. You can access an audit trail, trial balance, profit and loss account, balance sheet, budget and VAT account.

On line help is available in two ways. One source works in the same way as *Windows 95*. You can dial up help topics by subject or key words to invoke a short paragraph of helpful information. The second source of help is Sage's 'instant help' – this is a small window which remains on screen. It displays context sensitive help as you proceed through the program.

Many companies maintain websites which contain information useful to their customers. Sage is no exception. You can access the Sage website via the toolbar provided that you have a modem attached to the computer and a contract with an internet service provider like CompuServe, AOL etc.

The final option on the toolbar is the Tasks option. This is the electronic equivalent of a paper 'to do' list. You can remind yourself of the jobs that you should have done yesterday but didn't quite get round to!

A Look at the Ledgers

We haven't space in this book to look at the whole of the *Instant Accounting* program. However, we can take a quick look at three of the principal ledgers. These relate to customers, suppliers and internal accounts. By the way, don't be intimidated by the word 'ledgers'. In the old days, all accounts were maintained in big books called ledgers. Nowadays, of course, computerised accounts don't use ledgers. However, the term has stuck, so many accountants still talk about ledgers even though the 'ledgers' they are talking about are actually records stored electronically on a computer.

The Customer Module

Many packages call this the Sales Ledger which is the traditional name for the part of the accounting system dealing with sales administration. Nowadays, the term 'sales ledger' sounds a bit formal and archaic so Sage has labelled this part of the system the 'Customers' menu which sounds more user-friendly.

The 'Customers' part of the program will be of particular value to businesses which offer credit to their customers. Selling goods or services on credit involves a huge amount of administration. You have to maintain records of customers' names, addresses and credit balances. You have to chase debt with statements, letters and telephone calls.

Traditionally, businesses have managed credit sales manually using a Sales Day Book and Sales Ledger Cards. However, manual methods are really only viable if you have a very small number of credit customers to look after. Computerised sales records of the kind shown here are immeasurably more efficient. If you click the Customers icon in the main menu, you will be presented with the screen as shown below.

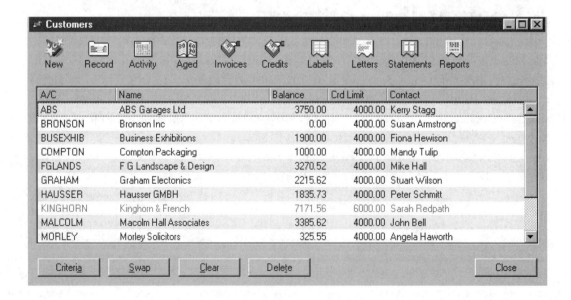

A/C	Name	Balance	Crd Limit	Contact
ABS	ABS Garages Ltd	3750.00	4000.00	Kerry Stagg
BRONSON	Bronson Inc	0.00	4000.00	Susan Armstrong
BUSEXHIB	Business Exhibitions	1900.00	4000.00	Fiona Hewison
COMPTON	Compton Packaging	1000.00	4000.00	Mandy Tulip
FGLANDS	F G Landscape & Design	3270.52	4000.00	Mike Hall
GRAHAM	Graham Electonics	2215.62	4000.00	Stuart Wilson
HAUSSER	Hausser GMBH	1835.73	4000.00	Peter Schmitt
KINGHORN	Kinghorn & French	7171.56	6000.00	Sarah Redpath
MALCOLM	Macolm Hall Associates	3385.62	4000.00	John Bell
MORLEY	Morley Solicitors	325.55	4000.00	Angela Haworth

Each of the subsidiary icons has a function as follows.

This Wizard helps you set up a new customer account. The customer account records the customer's name, address, telephone number, fax number, credit limit, credit period and any discount that you may have allowed that customer on their orders. If you are installing the accounts system from scratch, you will need to insert the customer's opening balance. Each customer must be allocated a unique customer reference number.

This option enables you to keep very comprehensive records about each customer. Not only will you have all of the basic information which you entered in the new customer wizard, you will gradually build a record of sales history as each month progresses. You can even fill in a blank 'memo' field where you can record detailed information about that customer's habits and preferences.

This option records invoices raised and customer payments for each customer. You can see at a glance the level of customer activity and tell how much debt is owed to you together with the debt's age.

This option enables you to print out an aged debt report for each customer. It is important to know which customers are paying their bills late so that you can chase them for their debts. The computer will scour your records for unpaid invoices and produce an outstanding debt list. The debt is broken down into columns showing how long the debt has been outstanding, eg 30 days overdue, 60 days overdue etc. Once you have identified delinquent customers, you can chase them for money. Some people find this listing alone pays for the introduction of a computerised accounting system.

A computer generated aged debt list is a real boon. Businesses relying on a manual system rarely produce the aged debt listings needed for good credit control.

This option enables you to enter invoices previously raised manually. Most people won't use this option. They will use the Invoices option on the main menu which enables you to generate an invoice within the program.

Invoices contain a great deal of detail which takes time to produce by hand. For example, each invoice must include:

- the customer's name and address
- your own name, address and VAT number
- a description of the goods or services
- the price, discount and VAT (where applicable)
- the date (and tax point date where necessary).

Much of this detail is stored permanently in the computer. When required, the information can be printed automatically onto the invoice thereby avoiding typing errors and saving time. Automated invoicing will help preserve your sanity!

The invoicing routines enable you to enforce credit limits. Each customer should have a credit limit beyond which they cannot stray. Whilst raising an invoice, the computer will check the amount of credit taken by each customer. If an order exceeds the customer's credit limit, the operator is warned with a message. Businesses without a computerised system may not have time to check each order as it arrives. The computerised system will perform credit checks automatically with no effort.

You may allow your customers a discount for buying in bulk or paying promptly or as an inducement to stay loyal to you. Once you have agreed the discount with your customer, the invoicing routines will automatically apply that discount to all future transactions. This means you don't get the arithmetic wrong or allocate the wrong discount to the wrong customer.

This option enables you to enter credit notes onto the system which have previously been produced manually. Most people will not use this option, they will use the Credit Notes option within 'Invoicing' on the main menu.

This option produces address labels for your customers. Your accounts system is a huge database of customer information. Why not use this database to send your customers letters containing details of special offers, price lists, promotions etc?

This option is particularly useful if you decide to write to customers telling them that they have overdue accounts. The software 'personalises' the stationery by automatically inserting the appropriate name, address and amount owed. Although letters can be a useful part of your credit control routine, you will probably still need to chase debts by telephone as well.

Sadly, not all customers pay their bills on time, some customers need a little prompting. A statement is a reminder to pay. Once again, the computer is on hand to help. Your accounts program will produce statements which summarise the amounts owed by each customer. Statements are difficult and time consuming to produce by hand. However, they can be produced automatically by a computerised system from data stored on the computer's hard disk. They are an invaluable part of credit control.

Instant Accounting comes preprogrammed with a range of useful sales reports. These include reports like Top Customer List, Customers over Credit Limit, Customers' Address List etc.

Summary

If you are involved in credit sales, you should consider installing the sales ledger first. It usually offers the biggest pay-off for the smallest amount of work. Indeed some people *only* install the computerised sales ledger, they continue to use manual methods for their remaining transactions.

Purchase Ledger

Sage Instant Accounting calls this part of the software the 'Suppliers' module which sounds more friendly than Purchase Ledger.

The Suppliers Ledger collects together details of purchases made by the business. If you buy a lot of goods or services on credit, you will benefit from the installation of a computerised purchase ledger. The purchase ledger keeps track of the amounts owed by you to your suppliers. Computerised purchase ledgers can:

- Generate an aged credit listing. This listing tells you how much you will have to pay each supplier in the coming weeks and months. This is a valuable guide when planning your cash outflows.

- Generate cheques. This looks impressive to your suppliers. With a computerised system, your bank account will be updated automatically at the same time.

- Generate supplier remittance advice notes automatically. This is especially useful if your supplier failed to include a remittance advice as part of their invoice to you.

- Your purchase ledger is a database of your suppliers. You can use it to stay in touch with them. Perhaps you may need to contact them to request quotations, or keep them in touch with your latest requirements.

Keeping an eye on purchases

The Sage Suppliers Ledger

Remember that the Suppliers Ledger is Sage's word for Purchase Ledger. If you select the Supplier ledger from the main menu, you are presented with the following screen.

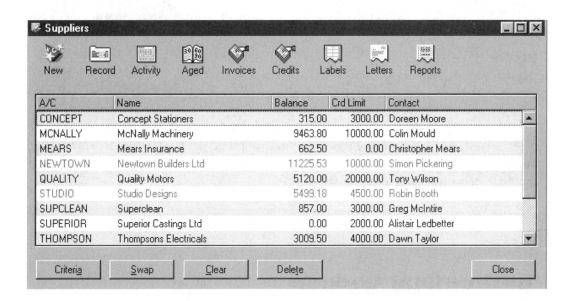

This is what the options within the Suppliers screen do.

Guides you through the set up for a new account.

Enables you to keep detailed records about suppliers including business name, address, contact name, terms of trade, history of transactions etc.

This option records the purchase history for that particular supplier.

Produces a report on how many days suppliers has been waiting for payment.

Enables you to enter a batch of purchase invoices into the computer.

Enables you to input suppliers' credit notes into the computer.

Enables you to produce name and address labels for your suppliers. Useful if you want to send them a circular.

Enables you to send them a 'form letter'. This is a standard letter which has been 'customised' by the addition of their name and address.

Instant Accounting includes a range of preprogrammed reports which most businesses will find useful. Examples include supplier address list, supplier activity, aged creditor analysis etc.

The Nominal Ledger

This is called the nominal ledger for purely historical reasons. Ledgers were originally books containing accounting records. The sales and purchase ledgers used to be called *personal* ledgers because they dealt with *people* who were suppliers or customers. The nominal ledger, on the other hand, deals with the business's own internal transactions. The nominal ledger is the heart of the system. All of the information about the business finds its way directly, or indirectly, into the nominal ledger.

Many business reports and accounts are produced from information contained within the nominal ledger. Examples include the Profit and Loss Account, Balance Sheet, budget reports and VAT reports.

If you select the Nominal Ledger option from the main menu, you will be presented with the following screen

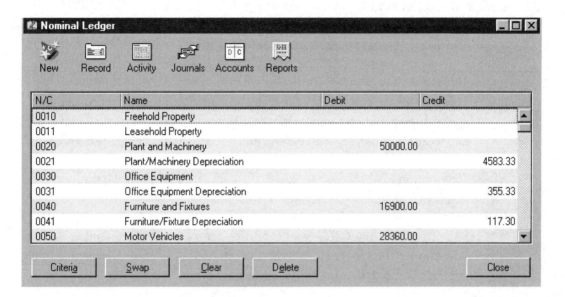

Notice that the window displays the types of income and expenditure recorded by Demonstration Exhibitions Ltd. If you scroll down the list, you will see the full range of account codes. Income and expenditure is coded because computers process coded account numbers more efficiently than text names. Here is a list of the account codes used in the program.

Account Code Range

Fixed Assets	0000–999
Current Assets	1000–1999
Current Liabilities	2000–2999
Capital and Reserves	3000–3999
Sales	4000–4999
Purchases	5000–5999
Direct Expenses	6000–6999
Overheads	7000–7999

The Nominal Ledger Sub Menus

This is what the Nominal Ledger icons do.

 The Wizard guides you through the setting up of a new nominal ledger account.

 This option is useful if you want to set up budgets. You can record last year's actual figure and this year's planned figure for each type of income and expenditure. This year's 'actual results' are added as the year proceeds.

 This option enables you to select an item of income or expenditure and display the account history so far this year.

 Sage operates under double entry book-keeping rules. This means that, if you choose the 'Journals' method of amending entries, you can modify accounts with debit and credit entries.

 If you select the Accounts icon followed by 'Edit', you will be able to see the account categories. If you select an overhead category, eg purchases in the left hand description column, you will be able to see a breakdown of that category on the right hand side of the screen.

 The *Instant Accounting* software arrives with built-in nominal ledger reports. These include reports covering nominal balances, nominal list, day books etc.

Information finds its way into the nominal ledger by one of the following routes.

Nominal Ledger Entries via the Sales Ledger

We have already said that sales details are kept in the sales ledger; however, a summary of these transactions is posted to the nominal ledger as each entry is made. The nominal ledger tracks sales by type of sale (A/c codes 4000 to 4999), the VAT associated with those sales (A/c 2200 Sales Tax Control A/c), and the total indebtedness of the customers (A/c 1100 Debtors Control A/c).

Nominal Ledger Entries via the Purchase Ledger

Details of purchase transactions are stored in the purchase ledger. A summary of these details are posted to the nominal ledger where they are recorded by type of expense, eg motor, rent, rates, materials etc. The ledger also records the total amount owed to trade creditors (A/c 2100 Creditors Control A/c) and the VAT associated with those purchases (A/c 2201 Purchase Tax Control A/c).

Nominal Ledger Entries via the Cashbook

Not all information reaching the nominal ledger arrives via the sales and purchase ledgers. Some entries arrive via the bank, cash and credit cards route. Under the rules of double entry, money movements are recorded both in the bank etc and the corresponding nominal ledger account.

Upgrading Your Software

An entry program such as *Instant Accounting* represents an ideal starting point for a business thinking of computerising its accounts. As the business grows, you can upgrade the software to include additional accounting functions like job costing, sales order processing, purchase order processing, fixed asset management etc.

Chapter 4

Choosing Your Software

In this book, we focus on the needs of small to medium sized businesses. Virtually every business of this size will buy its accounts software off the shelf. Large businesses may be able to afford bespoke accounting packages but smaller businesses are better served by the tried and tested mass market packages. Off-the-shelf packages are cheap, bug free and can be tailored to meet most business needs.

It is important to choose software which suits your business. Every business is different; for example, a retail shop has completely different accounting requirements to a building contractor. Some software packages are more suited to one kind of business than another. Although all the popular packages are good, you may find that one package suits your needs better than the others.

The right package?

Choose an accounts package appropriate for your accounting skills. A new business with a simple product range and limited accounting skills will be looking for a much simpler package than a business which has been established for 50 years, employs 100 people and trades with more than one country.

If you are not going to operate the package yourself, get the opinions of those members of staff who will. Your staff could think of important aspects which you haven't thought of. Staff involvement also generates a feeling of 'ownership' because everyone was involved in the choice.

Look for a package with good book-keeping routines which are intuitive to use. Make sure that the data entry screens are easy to understand. Check whether you can generate management reports which give *exactly* the information you need. Finally the package should provide the traditional accounts, these are the profit and loss account and balance sheet.

If you stick to the mainstream accounting packages, you will be hard put to find a bad product. Your choice is not so much between good and bad as between appropriate and inappropriate. Ironically, you will be making your choice when you are at your most inexperienced. If you aren't a computerised accounting expert, you need advice. You can get it from the following people:

- your accountant
- a computer dealer
- your business associates
- a business consultant.

For the moment, let's assume that you have asked a local computer dealer who specialises in accounts packages for help. On the one hand, *you* know all about your business but nothing about accounts packages. On the other hand, *the dealer* knows all about accounts packages and nothing about your business. Obviously, you and the dealer need to communicate so that, between you, you can find the right software for the business.

Your computer dealer can only sell you the *right* system if he knows how your business operates. Some dealers give you a checklist to complete. This checklist is important because it will narrow the choice of packages to those capable of doing the job. If you are given a checklist, be sure to complete it conscientiously. The right answers could save you a huge amount of wasted time later on!

If your dealer doesn't give you a checklist, have a look at the one on the next page. This will start you thinking about the accounting system you need.

What Package Do I Need?

- Are most of your transactions for cash or do you buy and sell on credit?
- Do you incur costs or expenses which are charged to your customers?
- Do you have several bank accounts?
- Do you deal in foreign currencies?
- Do you manufacture products from raw materials?
- Do you need to control stock ?
- How much of your capital is tied up in fixed assets?
- Do you need to accumulate the costs on specific jobs so that you can judge their profitability?
- How many customers do you have on your books at any one time?
- Do you offer discounts to customers?
- Do you have employees working for you?
- How many suppliers do you deal with at any one time?
- Do you have more than one company/business unit?
- Are managers responsible for control of their own costs?
- Are managers responsible for control of their own profitability?
- How many product lines do you have?
- Is each product unique or can it be allocated to meaningful broad categories?
- Will a single person be responsible for the accounting or will other people need access?
- Will more than one person need access at the same time?
- Will different parts of the accounting system be operated at the same time?
- How many transactions occur each month?
- How many expense headings will you need?

Continued overleaf

What Package Do I Need? (Contd)

- Do you need to analyse sales by product, salesman, territory etc?
- What is your VAT status?
- Do you operate any VAT retail schemes?
- Do you need to manage sales backlogs?
- Do you need to manage purchase backlogs?
- Do you have point-of-sale terminals?
- Do you want to check bank interest?
- Do you have subsidiaries?
- Do you need to generate despatch notes?
- How much accounting knowledge do you have?
- Do you want to generate invoices item by item or in batch mode.
- Do you need drill down? (ie analyse top numbers into detail automatically)
- Do you need help with bank reconciliation?

Beware the computer dealer who only knows one accounting package. Some dealers sell you the only package they understand regardless of whether it suits you or not.

It should not take long to narrow your choice down to one or two packages. At this point, ask if demonstration software is available. Try out the 'demo' and see if it feels right for you. Also talk to someone who has already installed the software. Check whether their experiences have been good or bad. Ask whether the software has been acredited by the Institute of Chartered Accountants in England and Wales (ICAEW). Also ask yourself:

- are the screens easy to understand?

- is data easy to enter?

- is the package intuitive to use?

- are self teach materials included in the package?

- is it easy to correct typing errors?

- does this package suit your kind of business?

- does the package offer guidance on transferring your manual data onto the computer?

- can you 'drill down'? (ie break top numbers down so you can see the detail which made them up).

Since your dealer and your accountant are likely to have a considerable influence on your decision, here are a few questions which you might like to put to them.

Questions for Your Dealer

- How long have you been trading?

- Do you specialise in any software?
  – what and why?

- What support staff do you have?
  – software
  – hardware

- What manufacturers products do you support?
  – software
  – hardware

Questions for Your Accountant

- Do you think I should computerise my accounts?

- How much will you charge to oversee the installation and set up of the program?

- Will computerised accounting reduce your fees?

- Do you foresee any particular problems for my business?

- Do you recommend any particular software?

- What accounting reports would you advise me to generate?

- What accounts coding structure should I use? (See Chapter 5 for an explanation of accounts coding).

- Do you have experience of installing computerised accounting software? Can you give me some examples?

Choosing the Right Hardware

Usually you specify the software first and then buy the hardware required to run it. This obviously makes sense if you have no computer to start with. On the other hand, if you already have a computer (perhaps used for word processing), check whether the old machine can also be used for your new accounting system. If not, you will have no choice but to buy a new computer.

It's very difficult to make a mistake buying computer hardware. Buy the most powerful machine that you can afford. Don't skimp on computer hardware. Never rely on minimum specifications. Buy considerably more memory, processor speed and disk space than the software recommends. You may even decide that you want to go up the range from the machine the salesman recommends. If you don't need your powerful computer for your current software, you will need it for the upgrade!

The real costs of computing are in *failing* to use the computer effectively – costs like:

- Information unavailable because no one knows how to run the relevant report.

- Information lost because the procedures for saving data were not understood.

- Information garbled because the significance of nominal ledger codes, cost centres or the dates of transactions was not understood.

Good hardware and software, together with comparatively cheap training (or the time taken to read manuals thoroughly), would save these costs.

It is ironic that some businessmen resent 'wasting' money on hardware or software when they cheerfully waste money on other business costs which would be eliminated if the system was functioning properly!

Chapter 5

Coding Your Accounts

You probably want to push straight on to the next chapter and start installing your software now. Don't do it! Before you touch the computer, there is one important area which you must get right. This is devising an accounts coding system. Let's explain what an accounts coding system is, and say why it is important.

Accounts software collects information and *organises* it. We need to collect our book-keeping information and organise it into some sort of 'filing system'. You can think of the 'filing system' rather like a bank of pigeon holes. Every time you collect a piece of information, you file it into the appropriate pigeon hole. That way, you always know how to get the information back again when you need it.

Life would be lovely if we could give each pigeon hole a nice long description like 'All the sales invoices we raised in May for D Childs & Sons'. Unfortunately, computers aren't very good at handling words and letters. However, they are brilliant at handling numbers! That is why our pigeon holes have to be labelled with numbers instead of descriptions. The numbers which are used to label the pigeon holes are based on our 'chart of accounts'.

Coding the chart of accounts is probably the most important single exercise you will undertake on your accounts package. If you get your accounts coding wrong, you won't be able to extract or sort the data that you need to run the business.

If you are not an accountant, you will probably need help to construct your chart of accounts. This is perfectly natural. Most people go into business because they have a knowledge of some kind of trade. Those with a knowledge of accounting go into the accounting trade, so it's hardly surprising that people running other businesses have only a hazy understanding of the financial side of things. Most businessmen are happy to pay to get their car serviced, but they may be reluctant to pay their accountant to advise on how the accounts coding system should be structured. If a business goes bust, it is more likely to be caused by the lack of financial information rather than the lack of transport! So don't be afraid to ask for help at this very important stage of the installation.

Working out your chart of accounts

Once the coding structure has been devised, it is difficult to change. Try to get it right first time. If you don't understand accounts coding, either

- use the default chart of accounts supplied with the package, or
- ask an experienced professional to devise a coding system which suits your business.

Don't allow novices to play with your coding structure or you will end up with a dud installation. Once you have drafted a code of accounts, circulate it to everyone who might have an interest in the outcome. This way your staff will pick up coding mistakes while it is still easy to correct them.

Why is the Chart of Accounts Important?

The chart of accounts is important because we need the chart of accounts to get information *out* of the computer. Let's illustrate this with an example. Suppose we want to keep an eye on our sales performance. If we put all our sales into one pigeon hole (using say code number 4000), we would only be able to extract our *total* sales at any one time. However, suppose we want more detail. Suppose, for example, that we want to know:

– what our sales figures were in the North of England or the South of England or Scotland or Wales
– how much of each product we sold in each area
– which salesmen sold the most products
– what type of customer bought our products; were they wholesalers, retailers, the general public etc.

We can only extract this information if we use a different code for each activity. For example, suppose we have account codes available between 4000 and 4999 to describe sales. We could use the first two digits to tell us which parts of the country received the products. For example:

40xx could be reserved for Southern England
41xx could be reserved for Northern England
42xx could be reserved for Scotland
43xx could be reserved for Wales
44xx could be reserved for other countries

We could reserve the last two digits to indicate which type of product was sold. For example, product X could be coded XX01. Product Y could be coded XX02. Product Z could be coded XX03 and so on. This means, for example, that code 4203 would record the value of product Z which has been sold in Scotland.

You can develop this idea to give access to any amount of information provided the information can be coded between the numbers 4000 to 4999.

Obviously, this logic doesn't just work for sales. You can use the same approach to monitor all sorts of income and expenditure.

How Much Detail do I Need?

You need to strike a balance when you code your accounts. On the one hand, you must code your accounts in sufficient detail to tell you all that you want to know. On the other hand, you don't want so much detail that you drive the data entry clerks mad with excessive codes – which nobody ever reads. You need a balance between effort and results. The level of detail will vary from one business to another. For example, one business may need a costing system which allocates wages to individual departments. Another business may be happy to record the total wages bill without ever worrying about the breakdown.

The Default Chart of Accounts

Most accounting packages come with a default chart of accounts. This default chart of accounts has been put together by the software house for a 'typical' business. The default chart of accounts is a valuable starting point for your deliberations. If you are lucky, you may be able to use the default chart exactly as it is. This will save you a lot of work.

A sample chart of accounts is shown on pages 50 to 53. This is the default taken from the *Sage Instant Accounting* accounts package. Don't panic! We know that there seems to be a lot of detail. However, once you understand the logic, you will find the whole system falls into place nicely.

Notice that the codes run from 0000 to 9999. This means that there are 10,000 possible 'pigeon holes' into which you can post information. Most businesses, of course, will only use a tiny fraction of the total number of account codes available.

You can see that the accounts are collected under the following headings:

- Fixed Assets
- Current Assets
- Current Liabilities
- Financed By
- Sales
- Purchases
- Direct Expenses
- Overheads
- Miscellaneous.

There are good reasons for these headings. They are required to produce a profit and loss account and balance sheet. They also provide a logical structure which enables you to produce key management reports (see Chapter 8 for more details).

Let's have a look at each of these headings in a little more detail.

Fixed Assets (Codes 0000 to 1000)

Have a look at the fixed assets examples on page 50. Fixed assets are assets bought for retention and use in the business. In the example, codes between 0000 and 1000 have been reserved for property, plant and machinery, office equipment, furniture and fittings and motor vehicles etc. The cost price of the asset is entered under the appropriate asset code, usually ending in the digit zero.

Fixed Assets

Note that each asset code has a linked depreciation account usually ending in the digit one. The depreciation accounts (ie these ending in 1 in our example) accumulate the depreciation charged over the life of the asset. This enables the written down value of the asset to be calculated at any time. The written down value is also called the 'book value'. The fixed asset part of the chart of accounts is used to produce asset information for the balance sheet, and depreciation figures for the profit and loss account.

You can add extra asset accounts by following the instructions in the user manual. Most small firms won't need to prepare management reports based on the fixed asset register because they won't have enough movement of high value items to make the effort worthwhile.

Current Assets (Codes 1001 to 2099)

Current assets are items owned by the business which will, ultimately, be sold to customers. Current assets include raw materials, work-in-progress, finished goods, stock. It also includes cash in hand and money in the bank. Current assets are important because some assets such as stock can tie up large amounts of money. You should definitely code your accounting system so that you can track current assets if you are a manufacturer, wholesaler or retailer. In the default system, current assets can be allocated codes between 1000 and 1999. The stock value of the current assets appears on the balance sheet. Usage of current assets is included in the 'cost of sales' figure on the profit and loss account.

You may want to produce management reports on current assets such as sales broken down by:

- type of stock
- length of time in stock
- value of stock etc.

Current Liabilities (Codes 2100 to 2999)

These are sums of money which you are 'liable' to pay in the near future. Accounting prudence dictates that you ought to have more current assets than current liabilities, otherwise you could be seriously embarrassed when the time comes to pay! Current liabilities include items like suppliers' invoices awaiting payment. They also include amounts of money owed to the VAT man, Inland Revenue or DSS etc.

Don't forget that you can have current liabilities even when you haven't received a bill! For example, you could have used two months' supply of gas or electricity. Even though you don't expect the bills until the end of the quarter, you are still 'liable' to pay for the amounts that you have consumed so far. Amounts owed in this way are called 'accruals'. Current liabilities on the default system are stored in account codes 2100 to 2999.

Financed By (Codes 3000 to 3999)

You will see these items when you print the annual accounts. Most businesses are started with money injected by the owners. The original capital can be supplemented by share issues, loans, overdrafts and profits retained in the business. This section of the accounts shows how the business has been financed.

Sales (Codes 4000 to 4999)

Nominal ledger codes for sales are allocated codes 4000 to 4999. There is considerable scope for ingenuity in sales coding. You may want to devise a coding structure which is capable of analysing sales by type, by area, or by sales representative for example.

Some of the items shown under 'sales' in the default chart of accounts have to be treated with caution. Sales of assets and insurance claims are 'income' in the most general sense but they are not actually 'sales' as entered on the profit and loss account. Check with your accountant that your software will treat these items correctly from an accounts point of view.

Purchases (Codes 5000 to 5999)

Codes 5000 to 5999 are available to record 'purchases'. You may remember that much of the data contained in the nominal ledger comes via the purchase ledger. Remember the word 'purchases' has a very specific meaning in the world of accounting. Purchases are items bought for resale. Purchases does not include items bought for retention and use within the business, these are called fixed assets. You may wish to code purchases so that they can be charged to a particular budget. This will enable you to keep track of who is spending the business' money. Purchases could well be the subject of a key management report (see later).

Purchases

Direct Expenses (Codes 6000 to 6999)

These are expenses 'directly' associated with producing the goods or performing the service which you offer your customers. For manufacturers, this category will obviously include production expenses which can be broken down into as many sub codes as you choose. Check with your accountant which of the codes between 6000 to 6999 should be entered as 'direct expenses' for your business and which should be entered as 'overheads' (see below).

Overheads (Codes 7000 to 7999)

These are items of expenditure which are *not* directly associated with producing the product or providing the service. Overheads tend to be incurred irrespective of the level of business activity, eg depreciation, rates, rents, insurance etc. The default set of accounts uses account codes 7000 to 7999 for overheads. This gives you up to 1000 pigeon holes to record overheads! Obviously, you need to strike a balance between the number of categories you create and the effort required to code expenditure across all of these categories.

Miscellaneous (Codes 8000 to 9999)

The miscellaneous items shown in the default chart of accounts can be treated like overheads.

Checking Your Chart of Accounts

Once you have coded your accounts, take a printout and give a copy to everyone who needs to enter, or use, data from the accounts system. Check that you have all of your reporting categories covered by an accounts code. Also give a copy to managers who use the output from the accounts system to generate key management reports. Check that the categories you have chosen are capable of providing the information at the level that they need. Print out a further, revised copy whenever you add or subtract categories. This will save endless confusion should people try to code data into accounts which you no longer use, or into accounts which have been split into a range of more detailed codes.

Only you can decide how many codes you need. Too much detail can be as big a headache as too little. This is particularly so if vast amounts of time are spent coding income and expenditure to produce lots of reports – which nobody reads. On the other hand, it won't be possible to extract meaningful information if the analysis is not detailed enough – which was probably the reason you installed the accounts system in the first place!

The Sage Default Nominal Ledger

Here is a list of the accounts in the default Sage nominal ledger.

Fixed Assets

0010 Freehold Property
0011 Leasehold Property
0020 Plant and Machinery
0021 P/M Depreciation
0030 Office Equipment
0031 O/E Depreciation
0040 Furniture and Fittings
0041 F/F Depreciation
0050 Motor Vehicles
0051 M/V Depreciation

Current Assets

1001 Stock
1002 Work-in-Progress
1003 Finished Goods
1100 Debtors Control Account
1101 Sundry Debtors
1102 Other Debtors
1103 Prepayments
1200 Bank Current Account
1210 Bank Deposit Account
1220 Building Society Account
1230 Petty Cash

Current Liabilities

2100 Creditors Control Account
2101 Sundry Creditors
2102 Other Creditors
2109 Accruals
2200 Tax Control Account
2210 VAT Liability
2210 PAYE
2211 National Insurance
2230 Pension Fund
2300 Loans
2310 Hire Purchase
2320 Corporation Tax
2330 Mortgages

Financed By

3000	Ordinary Shares	3101	Undistributed Reserves
3001	Preference Shares	3200	Profit and Loss Account
3100	Reserves		

Sales

4000	Sales Type A	4900	Miscellaneous Income
4001	Sales Type B	4901	Royalties Received
4002	Sales Type C	4902	Commissions Received
4009	Discounts Allowed	4903	Insurance Claims
4100	Sales Type D	4904	Rent Income
4101	Sales Type E	4905	Distribution and Carriage
4200	Sales of Assets		

Purchases

5000	Materials Purchases	5100	Carriage
5001	Materials Imported	5101	Duty
5002	Miscellaneous Purchases	5102	Transport Insurance
5003	Packaging	5200	Opening Stock
5009	Discounts Taken	5201	Closing Stock

Direct Expenses

6000	Productive Labour	6201	Advertising
6001	Cost of Sales Labour	6202	Gifts and Samples
6002	Sub-contractors	6203	PR (Lit & Brochures)
6100	Sales Commissions	6900	Miscellaneous Expenses
6200	Sales Promotions		

Overheads

7001	Directors' Salaries	7404	Overseas Entertaining
7002	Directors' Remuneration	7405	Overseas Travelling
7003	Staff Salaries	7406	Subsistence
7004	Wages – Regular	7500	Printing
7005	Wages – Casual	7501	Postage and Carriage
7006	Employer's NI	7502	Telephone
7007	Employer's Pension	7503	Telex/Telegram/Facsimile
7008	Recruitment Expenses	7504	Office Stationery
7100	Rent	7505	Books etc
7102	Water Rates	7600	Legal Fees
7103	General Rates	7601	Audit & Accountancy Fees
7104	Premises Insurance	7602	Consultancy Fees
7200	Electricity	7603	Professional Fees
7201	Gas	7700	Equipment Hire
7202	Oil	7701	Office Machine Maintenance
7203	Other Heating Costs	7800	Repairs and Renewals
7300	Fuel and Oil	7801	Cleaning
7301	Repairs and Servicing	7802	Laundry
7302	Licences	7803	Premises Expenses (Misc)
7303	Vehicle Insurance	7900	Bank Interest Paid
7304	Misc Motor Expenses	7901	Bank Charges
7400	Travelling	7902	Currency Charges
7401	Car Hire	7903	Loan Interest Paid
7402	Hotels	7904	HP Interest
7403	UK Entertaining	7905	Credit Charges

Miscellaneous

8000	Depreciation	8201	Subscriptions
8001	Plant/Machinery Depreciation	8202	Clothing Costs
8002	Furniture/Fix/Fittings Depn	8203	Training Costs
8003	Vehicle Depreciation	8204	Insurance
8004	Office Equipment Depreciation	8205	Refreshments

Miscellaneous (Contd)

8100	Bad Debt Write Off		9998	Suspense Account
8102	Bad Debt Provision		9999	Mispostings Account
8200	Donations			

Summary

Before you computerise your accounting system, you need a pretty clear idea of what you are trying to achieve.

- Put the effort into the planning stage.

- Your chart of accounts is key to the successful operation of your system.

- Try to produce an accounts structure which is simple, logical and flexible. This will enable you to enter data easily and get reports which tell you what you really need to know.

- Get advice from your accountant/computer dealer.

- Get it right first time! Nobody wants to install a computerised accounting system twice – once is quite enough!

Chapter 6

Installing a New System

If you computerise a mess, you will end up with a computerised mess. A computerised mess is even more of a problem than a manual mess. It is worthwhile tidying up your manual records and procedures before you computerise. That way, you don't try to introduce a new system whilst ironing out the bugs in the old one!

You have probably been keeping your records in an analysed cashbook along the lines suggested in *Simple and Practical Book-keeping* (which is another book in this series).

Here are some things to do before you install your computer system.

- Get your paper filing system up to date. Ensure that you can locate your sales and purchase invoices, bank statements, wages records, petty cash records etc.

- Get your 'standing records' in good shape before you go 'live'. Standing records are records which don't change from day to day. They include things like customers' names, addresses, telephone numbers and credit limits, suppliers' names and addresses and credit limits, product categories and price lists etc. These can be transferred onto the computer before you enter any balances. It is much easier to transfer 'clean' records. It will take forever if they have to be checked as they are entered into the computer.

- Make sure that your account balances are brought up to date before they are entered into the computer. If you start off with the wrong balances, you will introduce mistakes into the accounts before you have even begun!

- Make sure that your accounts coding is sensible and agreed by everyone who needs to either enter data, or produce reports. Set the computer up so that the account codes are grouped in such a way as to produce a profit and loss account and balance sheet when required. This will have been done automatically if you use the default set of accounts.

- Choose a logical start date; the most obvious time would be the start of a new accounting year. If this isn't convenient, perhaps you could start at the beginning of a new VAT quarter or a new reporting quarter for the business. If you have no significant milestones in mind, at least choose a start date which coincides with a month end.

Making a Start

Don't try and do everything on day one – it simply won't work! Do as much preparation beforehand as you can. Enter all the standing information into the computer well in advance of the start date. Transfer your opening balances to the computer on day one. Don't try to run up the whole of the accounting suite on the start date. Choose the most important module and work on that one. You won't have enough staff (or knowledge) to install every possible module on day one. Most modules in a computerised accounting suite work perfectly well as stand alone modules.

You will probably want to start with the Sales Ledger since this offers most 'bang for the buck'. Once installed, you will soon be able to:

- generate accurate invoices
- master customer credit accounts
- send statements automatically
- produce an aged debt list which will help you chase payment
- provide a customer list which may be useful to your sales force.

Firms where most of the accounting workload is sales related may never get any further than installing the Sales Ledger. This would be a shame but there is no rule which says you have to install every part of the package!

For firms with more than half a dozen staff, the next most logical step may be to introduce the computerised payroll. This module will save hours of tedious calculation but doesn't have to be linked up to the rest of the accounting system from day one. Gradually you will be able to commission all of the modules in the accounting suite which you plan to use. Most businesses will install the sales ledger, purchase ledger and nominal ledger early on. This is because they are the backbone of integrated accounting systems. Once the 'basic' modules are running, you can add other modules like job costing, bill of materials, stock control, sales order processing, purchase order processing etc. A phased installation will enable you to cope with change slowly.

Don't be afraid to ask for outside help. To begin with, you will probably be constantly on the phone to the software house's 'help-line'. A first year subscription will pay for itself many times over. It will enable you to cope with the 'nuts and bolts' of the package. You may also need to ask your accountant or computer dealer for help at some stage. There's nothing like a friendly face when wrestling with the complexities of a new-fangled computer system! Their experience with previous customers should mean that they can solve your problem quickly and easily.

Parallel Running

You may be lucky and find that the new system 'beds down' immediately. However, this doesn't happen every time. This is why most people keep the old manual system running alongside the new system for a period of time. This period is called parallel running, it lasts as long as it takes to get confidence in the new system; it could be a few weeks or it could be many months. Parallel running is a real chore since the extra effort of running

Parallel running?

two systems – one of which is new and unproved – can place a huge workload on accounting staff. Try to choose a quiet time of the year to take your first tentative steps into the world of computerised accounts!

Training

However well set up a new system is, it will represent a change from the old system. You will have to spend time learning how the new system works. Here are some ideas.

- Check whether your computerised accounting package has a tutorial. This will give you valuable 'hands-on' experience before attempting the real thing. Using the tutorial could save you time in the long run.

- Get some training! If you don't teach people how to do things right, you have only yourself to blame if they do things wrong. Invest some cash in training your staff so that they can operate the system effectively. They need to be able to recognise

Training may help!

mistakes when they occur and be able to correct them as the need arises.

- Train backup staff so that the system does not grind to a halt when your main operator is on holiday or leaves.

- Don't neglect your own training! If everyone in the company understands the accounting system except you, you have lost control of the business. Remember, achieving greater control was the object of the exercise in the first place.

Viruses

A great deal of newspaper ink has been spilt warning about the risk of virus infections. In practice, the risks may be less than is popularly believed. Nevertheless, virus infection is simple to guard against and should be included in your range of protective measures taken when installing the accounting system. Here are some ideas.

- Install an anti-virus checker, preferably one that operates in the background, constantly checking for new virus arrivals.

- Don't allow people to load pirate software onto the accounts computer, especially if it is from a dodgy area like an Internet download.

- If possible, keep the accounts computer off the general office network. This could prevent cross infection from machines over which the accounts staff have no control.

- Restrict physical access to the accounts machines so people can't walk into the accounts office out of working hours and 'play' with the system.

- Virus check incoming floppy discs on another computer before they are loaded onto the accounts system. Some people keep an old outdated PC specifically for this purpose.

Protecting Sensitive Information

The Data Protection Act requires sensitive information stored on computers to be protected from distribution to the world at large. If you have installed a payroll program, restrict access to the payroll program with password protection. Your payroll data may include sensitive personal information. Register with the Data Protection Registrar.

In addition to the payroll program, you may need to password protect other parts of the accounts software. For example, a disaffected employee could print your customer list and give (or sell) it to your competitors. If sensitive data is only made available to those who need it, this will prevent the leakage of valuable information.

Employing the Right Accounts Staff

Computerised accounting will operate better if under the control of trained and conscientious staff. Accounts staff need to be honest, numerate and computer literate. They need to be able to understand, and follow, the company's procedures. New staff should be given training or given time to read the manuals, or work through the tutorials that come with most accounting software. Where possible, staff should be encouraged to learn other parts of the system, not just the part they normally work on. This means that, if one person is sick, the whole department won't grind to a halt.

Able to Deal With the Euro

It is not generally appreciated that accounting systems will need to be able to handle both pounds and the Euro when Britain joins the single European Currency. It may be worth making sure that the program you are installing has this facility built in. It will be worth checking the way the system works *prior* to Britain's joining day because some of your customers may want to conduct their business in Euros instead of pounds.

Able to Deal With the Year 2000

So much has been written about the Millennium bug that there is no need to expand on it here. Make sure that the hardware and the software you install will be able to recognise the year 2000. Most reputable software houses had a 'year 2000 fix' in place well before the year 2000. That leaves you to check that your hardware can cope with the new Millennium. You also need to check that any program which you have *linked* to your accounting suite, like spreadsheets, word processors, databases or marketing software which 'talks' to the accounts programme can also handle the change.

Paperwork

If anything, computers tend to generate more paperwork than the manual system they replace. In general, therefore, the paperless office is a myth. You will probably find it worthwhile making month-end print outs. That way, you will still be able to function if the computer stops working for any reason. Your auditor will want to see a print out of the audit trail. This is a list of all of the transactions which have taken place so far in the current accounting year.

The paperless office?

Accepting Change

The introduction of a new system tends to change more than the mechanics of operating the system. Computerisation means that information is handled in a different way. Access to information is granted to those who can operate the computer, rather than to those with the key to the safe or filing cabinet. It may be denied to those who cannot operate the computer or who do not know the password. Cheques may be generated independently of the person who controls the cheque book. Errors can be made which have never been made before. New procedures will be needed which find and correct these new types of errors.

Installing and operating a first class computerised accounting package represents something of a challenge. However, it is people who solve problems not computers. You will have to manage the computer if it is to be useful. By the same token, computers do not create problems. Like any tool, if they are used with insufficient knowledge or skill or in inappropriate circumstances, they may end up being part of the problem rather than part of the solution.

Success!

Chapter 7

Controls, Routines and Procedures

This chapter describes the kind of precautions that you need to take to ensure that your accounting system stays up and running.

Backing up Your Data

Imagine arriving at work one day to discover that your computer has been stolen or burnt in a fire! Alternatively, how would you feel if your hard disk failed and you lost all your data!

These are just two of the disasters awaiting those who don't have backup routines. In this section, we will examine some precautions which will protect your accounts system, not only physically but also from a data integrity point of view.

If you lose your data, you will have to regenerate it from scratch. The consequences of this are too horrible to bear thinking about. You must have a backup system which minimises this exposure.

You need to decide how often to back up your data. It could be once an hour, once a day, once a week or once a month depending on how much data you enter. Most people back up their data once a day because it gets them into a routine. Daily backups also strike a balance between the effort of backing up and the risk of data loss.

Don't restrict yourself to a single set of backup disks. Data can become corrupt without you being aware of it. This means that your single set of backup disks may restore data which is only slightly less corrupt than the data already on the system!

The best system of backups is called the grandfather, father, son system. This is so called because you maintain three generations of backup. Have a look at the diagram on the next page. Notice on the top line that you keep one backup disk for each day of the week. These daily disks are recycled so that each Monday you overwrite data from the previous Monday. This means that you have a whole week's worth of daily backups available at any time.

The second row of the diagram shows the weekly disks. Every Friday you should make not one, but *two* Friday disks. Put the second Friday disk to one side. Since there are either four or five Fridays in a month, you will need to keep five *extra* Friday disks in circulation. These weekly disks (taken every Friday) mean that, even if there is a disaster with the daily disks, you should never have to go back further than a week to reconstruct your accounts system. As you start each new month, you overwrite the old weekly disks from the previous month.

Beneath the weekly disks in the illustration sit the monthly disks. You keep one backup disk for each past month. The monthly backup is taken on the last working day of the month. That way, you can go back to a previous month's position should you ever need to do so.

Although the grandfather, father, son system means that you have a lot of backup disks, it is worth it because backup disks are cheap. Regenerating data costs the earth! This system gives you 'belt and braces' protection against loss of data, however and whenever that loss happens.

We have shown backups on floppy disks. Naturally, you can back up onto whatever media you choose. It could be floppy disks, tapes, zip disks or even recordable CDs. It is worth keeping some backup disks off-site in case a fire destroys both the computer and the backups!

There is no point in backing up data if you can't restore it. Make an attempt to restore from your backup disks to another (non accounting) computer some time just to make sure that you could use the backup disks in a real emergency.

How to Backup onto Floppy Disks

Daily Backups

Weekly Backups

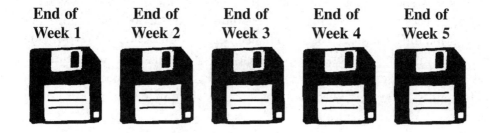

Monthly Backups

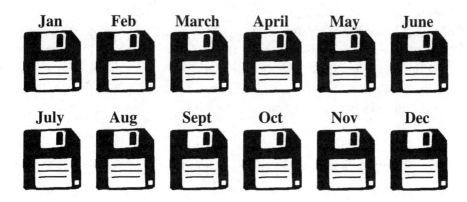

Monthly Routines

A system of daily backups will help protect you from a major physical loss of data but it isn't enough, you need to ensure that your accounts data is correct. For example:

- How do you know if your data entry is up-to-date?
- Have your direct debits been entered in the accounts properly this month?
- Do your bank records agree with the bank statement?
- Does the physical cash in hand agree with the amount shown in the accounts?
- Has your data been entered correctly?
- Are your VAT records correct?

These, and many other issues, are checked during the 'month-end routine'. Just as most businesses choose to backup data daily, most businesses choose to check the integrity of their accounts monthly. There is nothing magical about a monthly period. However, a monthly routine strikes a balance between the amount of work entailed and the degree of control it generates. The end of each month is also a natural break-point at which to review the month's activities. Many items of income and expense are paid monthly. Here are the controls you need to introduce to make sure that your accounting system stays healthy.

Complete the Month's Transactions

You will normally enter transactions into the system as the month progresses. However, we suggest you have a good hunt around at the end of each month to make sure that *all* sales and purchase invoices have been entered into the system. Have any bills been left in the pending tray awaiting clarification? Month-end is the time to make sure that every item has been sorted out and entered.

You may also decide that month-end is a good time to complete your payments to your suppliers. Make sure that all payments are actioned and entered into the accounting system.

Recurring Entries

Most businesses have recurring entries such as standing orders for rent, mortgage, hire purchase, lease payments etc. Check whether these payments have been included in the month's accounting entries. Also keep an eye on quarterly and half-yearly standing orders, make sure that these have been included in your accounts.

Reconcile the Bank Account

Each month check that what you think you have in the bank is what the bank thinks you have in the bank! Differences could arise because:

- The bank's accounts show entries not in your records, eg:
  - bank charges
  - direct debits which you have forgotten to enter in your cashbook
  - bank automated clearing service (BACS) payments into your account for which you had no notification
  - bank mispostings.

- Your records could show entries which have not appeared in your bank account. Normally these will be unpresented cheques or deposits made too late in the day to appear on that day's bank statement.

- Mistaken entries in your records, eg entering the wrong figures, transposing numbers etc.

Ask your bank to send you a bank statement at the end of every month. When you receive your bank statement, 'tick back' all the bank's entries against the entries in your computer. This should reveal any discrepancies. This process is so important that most accounts systems build in a routine to help you reconcile the bank account.

This is how you reconcile your bank account with *Instant Accounting*.

From the main menu, select 'Bank Accounts'. From the Bank menu, highlight the account you want to reconcile.

Select the 'Record' tab. Make sure that the 'No Bank Reconciliation' box is left unticked, as shown below.

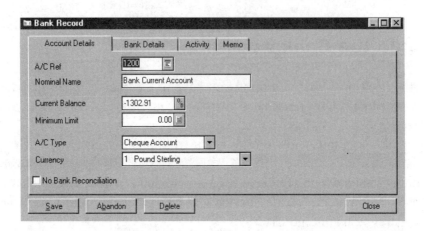

Return to the Bank Accounts menu and press the 'Reconcile' key. You will see a screen similar to that shown below.

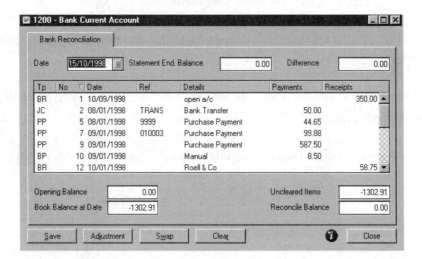

Check each entry on your bank statement and highlight the matching entry in the Bank Reconciliation window. Notice how the 'Difference' box changes to reflect each new amount highlighted. When you have reconciled your records with the bank's records, press 'Save'. This will prevent the reconciled items from reappearing next time you want to check your next bank statement.

Reconciling Cash

Businesses which deal with other businesses tend to make their payments via BACS or cheque. they deal with very little cash. On the other hand, businesses which sell to the general public can still collect a lot of cash.

If your business does deal in cash, you should reconcile your cash in hand with the accounting records. This makes sure that you can account for cash received and cash paid out. If the two don't agree then you have probably made one or more of the following mistakes.

- Someone has paid out cash without any entry being made in the computer.
- Someone has received cash without any entry being made in the computer.
- The entries in the computer have been made with the wrong figures, eg numbers transposed or misread.
- Giving and receiving the wrong change.

If you don't find any mistakes or omissions to acount for the discrepancy, it may be caused by theft.

How much cash should you have in hand at the end of the month? Your computer will calculate this as:

	Opening cash brought forward
add	Cash in
less	Cash out
equals	Closing cash balance carried forward.

If the cash in hand matches the balance in the computer then everything is fine. If not, we need to do some detective work. For example:

- Have all the entries in the computer been entered correctly?
- Was the opening balance figure brought forward from the last month correct?
- Has anyone 'borrowed' any money?
- Can anyone remember anything happening which may have caused the mistake?

If the worst comes to the worst and you can't agree the cash in hand with the computer, you will have to adjust the carry forward figure to reflect the actual amount of cash in the till. You can write off the difference to 'mispostings' account. Too many mistakes are symptoms of carelessness on someone's part. Perhaps you should look at the way cash is handled. You may need to change the way money is handled. This month's closing balance is carried forward to become next month's opening cash balance.

Accounting Adjustments

Most accounting progams print out a Profit and Loss Account and Balance Sheet on demand. People normally print out the set of accounts as part of the month-end routine. Be aware, however, that the figures generated by your program may not be completely accurate. This is because a 'true' set of accounts contains adjustments for:

- accruals
- prepayments
- depreciation of fixed assets
- stock adjustments
- work-in-progress adjustments.

These adjustments are explained in *Simple and Practical Accounting* which is another book in this series.

Of course, you may be happy to use the unadjusted accounts to give you a rough guide to business performance. If you want to incorporate the adjustments shown above, you will need to make journal entries using the 'Journal Entries' option contained within the 'Nominal Ledger'.

The Journal Entries screen is shown below.

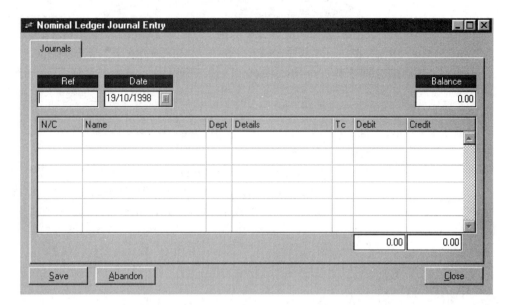

The accounting background behind these adjustments are really beyond the scope of this book. However, here is a quick outline of the journal entries you need to make. Chapter 11 contains some quick guidance on double entry. This may be useful if you are not too sure about 'debits' and 'credits'.

Accruals

Accruals are amounts entered into the accounts to provide for expenses incurred but not yet billed to you (eg electricity bills). The estimated accrual is a debit to the expense category with a corresponding credit to the accruals account.

Prepayments

Prepayments are amounts paid out *before* you receive the product or service (eg car tax and insurance). The entries are a debit entry to the prepayments accounts and a credit entry to the expense category involved.

Depreciation

Depreciation is the reduction in value of an asset due to wear and tear or technical obsolescence. The entries are credit the depreciation account for the fixed asset concerned and debit the profit and loss depreciation account.

Stock Adjustments

If your stock value fluctuates widely from month to month then these changing stock levels could distort your profit figure. If this is the case, you will need to build stock valuation into your profit and loss account. Do this by debiting your opening stock and crediting your closing stock each month.

Work-in-Progress

Work-in-progress represents the value of work done for customers which you have not yet been able to bill to them. The journal entries are the same as for stock.

Month End Procedures

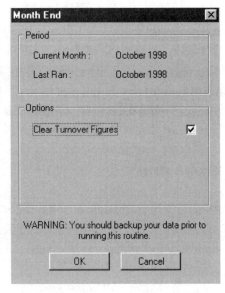

Instant Accounting has a built-in month-end procedure. Before running month-end, check that the program date is set to the last working day of the month. Open the 'Tools' menu and select 'Period End'. From the 'Period End' option, select 'Month End'. This will give the month-end screen as shown on the right.

Mark the 'clear turnover figures' box so that your reports show the balance for the current month only. If each month is not cleared down as the year progresses, your monthly reports will show cumulative amounts each time.

File Maintenance

From the 'File' menu, select 'Maintenance'. From the 'Maintenance' menu, select 'Error Checking'. The File Maintenance screen is shown below. Even though you will normally run error checking prior to your daily backup, you will still want to do this as part of month end.

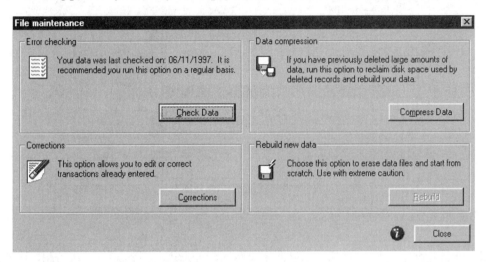

The error checking routine should warn you of errors early enough to fix them before they corrupt your data.

Print and Reconcile the VAT Return Analysis

(**Note** *You may feel safer if you take a backup before you calculate and reconcile your VAT return. The process of reconciliation 'clears' your current VAT entries. In the case of mistake, you may want to return to the pre-VAT reconciled records so that you can repeat the reconciliation using your backup data should the VAT return analysis proves wrong for any reason).*

Normally you will report VAT quarterly. On a VAT quarter day (which is, of course, normally a month end day), proceed as follows. From the main menu, select 'Financials'. From the Financials menu, select 'VAT'.

This will give you the screen shown below.

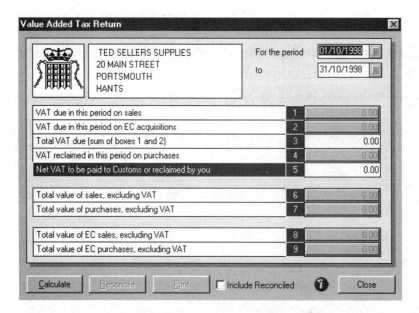

Make sure that the dates at the top right-hand corner of the screen properly reflect the VAT period for which you are accounting. Press the 'Calculate' button shown on the bottom left-hand part of the screen. This will fill in the VAT return for you. Print the VAT return and then, if happy with the result, press the 'Reconcile' button which will flag the items which have been included in this VAT return.

Print Reports

You can print as many (or as few) monthly reports as you choose. Since reports are available from a computerised accounting system on demand, you don't have to wait for month-end to generate them. However, many businesses run routine month-end management reports. Quite often accountants want to keep reports showing the state of play on the last day of each accounting month for the past year. The choice is yours. If the computer ever fails for some reason, you may be pleased to have a set of month-end reports to fall back on. This will help you to keep the business running while you get the computer back up again.

Here is a list of some of the reports you may like to consider:

- Audit Trail
- Trial Balance
- Aged Analysis for debtors and creditors
- Statements
- Profit and Loss Account and Balance Sheet
- Key Management Reports (covered in the next chapter).

Backup the Data

Backup your data as described previously, clearly labelling the disks (or tapes) as 'after month-end' for the particular month concerned.

Year End

At the end of every accounting year, you need to do a 'year-end'. This will be used to produce your annual accounts. Unless you are particularly competent at accounts, we suggest you perform a normal month-end routine and then invite your accountant to complete the year-end adjustments for you.

Most accountants are familiar with accounting packages. You could book a visit from your accountant 10–14 days after year-end. This 10–14 day delay will give you time to enter last minute data. Your accountant can then make the year-end adjustments, produce the final adjusted accounts, and return the program to your control. You will then be ready to start your new financial year confident that your accounts data is in a good shape.

Chapter 8

Management Reporting

When you originally decided to install a computerised accounting program, you probably had two main benefits in mind. These may have been:

- **Improved administration**
  - better systems for handling book-keeping, value added tax, invoicing, debt collection, wages etc.

- **Access to management information**
  - profit and loss account, balance sheet, management reports, budgets etc.

In this chapter, we will focus on the second benefit, which is access to management information.

Management reporting is so much easier on a computer! Manual systems require so much time and effort to maintain that there isn't enough labour left to *analyse* the information that has been collected. Computerised accounts provide management reports automatically at virtually no effort. This is a very important benefit.

Management accounts fall into three main categories.

- **Traditional accounts:**
  - profit and loss
  - balance sheet.

- **Key Management reports covering areas such as:**
  - sales performance analysis
  - cost breakdown
  - wage costs analysis
  - debtors and creditors position
  - bank and cash position.

- **Budget reports:**
  - actual versus planned income and expenditure for the year.

Let's have a look at these reporting categories in a little more detail.

Traditional Accounts

The Profit and Loss Account and Balance Sheet

You need to know whether the business is profitable. This information is, of course, given in the profit and loss account. The balance sheet is also valuable because it summarises what the business owns, what it owes *to* others and how much it is owed *by* others.

Most accounting software produces a profit and loss account and balance sheet. We mentioned in an earlier chapter that it helps to have a little accounting knowledge when producing these reports. This is because a 'proper' set of accounts should include adjustments for prepayments, accruals, depreciation, stock levels etc.

Be careful when reading accounts. Many small businesses are not too careful about separating the owner's private expenditure from business expenditure! A properly constructed set of accounts should have all expenditure of a personal nature purged from the business accounts. Private expenditure includes items such as private mileage, private use of telephone, personal items bought via the business etc.

Be careful if you decide to modify your income or expense categories. When the computer assembles your accounts, it collects together categories of income and expense based *entirely* on the accounts codes assigned to them. If you create a new accounting code and assign it to the wrong accounts category, you will get a false impression of profitability.

Key Management Reports

People attending 'Accounting for Non Accountants' courses often leave with the impression that financial reporting begins and ends with the profit and loss account and balance sheet. **This is not the case**. Valuable as they are, these numbers only give a broad brush indication of business performance as a whole. The overall profit figure is important to the owners, directors and chief accountant. However, the other managers in the business need much more detailed information about the income/expenditure in the area of the business within their control. For example, the sales manager will want to know the sales figures in considerable detail. He may want to know sales by:

- month
- customer name
- product line
- sales representative
- geographic area
- industry sector etc.

These detailed management reports are called key management reports because they deal with important (or 'key') areas of the business. You can create a key management report for any aspect of the business which you consider important.

Many of these key management reporting requirements are so well established that most accounting programs provide them pre-programmed into the system. This is a valuable time saver. For example, the *Sage Instant Accounting* sales ledger comes pre-programmed with reports on:

- aged debtors analysis
- top customer list
- credit limit exceeded
- customer account history

- customer list
- sales day books
- sales turnover by month
- sales by analysis code
- profit report by customer
- outstanding sales order
- back order list.

If the report you want has not been pre-programmed for you, you can use the in-built report generator to produce your own. You will be able to generate virtually any report you want *provided you have coded your accounts data correctly.*

Every business is different so each business will have its own particular key indicators. However, here are some of the key management reports available in *Instant Accounting*, in addition to the ones covering sales shown above.

Purchase Ledger Reports

Aged creditor analysis
Daily purchases report
Purchases day books summary
Purchase account histories
Supplier activity
Supplier address list
Top supplier
Outstanding purchase orders

Nominal Ledger Key Reports

Departmental analysis
Nominal account balances
Nominal account history
Nominal ledger budget v actual
Nominal list
Trial balance

Bank Reports

Current account history
Deposit account history
Petty cash
Credit card payments and receipts

Product Reports

Product categories
Product parts explosion
Product prices
Product profit
Re-order levels

Financial Reports

Audit trail
Balance sheet
Profit and loss account
Budget report
Departmental analysis
VAT position.

Budgets

Budgeting is an important element of financial control. Each year the owners or directors of the business set overall targets for the coming year. These targets can involve a broad variety of intentions like:

- raise sales by 10 per cent
- increase profitability by a third
- start selling in a new market etc.

None of these intentions has any teeth unless responsibility for that activity is delegated to an individual. Budgeting achieves this objective. It takes top numbers and breaks them down so that control of every aspect of the business is delegated to a single manager. That manager's performance is then reviewed periodically to see whether his (or her) part of the plan is being achieved.

Obviously generating and controlling budgets can create a mountain of paperwork. Fortunately, the computer helps us to bring this under control. A good computerised accounting system will have budget routines built in. Provided that you have devised a logical accounts coding structure, these budget routines will go to work for you from day one.

The computer will store each manager's targets for the months ahead. As each month unfolds, the computer will accumulate data to check whether that manager is on target.

Most standard accounting software provides an overall profit budget. Whilst these overall profit numbers are useful, they are not nearly as useful as budgets broken down by department. *Instant Accounting* does provide the ability to break down business activities into departments. You may prefer to show budget expenditure based on cash expenditure rather than the adjusted expenditure used for profit reporting purposes. Profit figures are more difficult to calculate, and most people understand cash movements more easily than profit movements. This is because the finer points of accounting theory are not understood by everyone.

If you don't need budgets when you start, you will probably need them a couple of years downstream. Fortunately, most packages offer you a cheap and simple version which you can cut your teeth on. You can then upgrade at a later date when it suits you.

Summary

In Chapter 2, we set out to get control of our money. You may remember that we wanted to know:

- How much money have we got?
- Where has it come from?
- Where does it go to?
- How much money am I owed?
- How much money do I owe others?
- Am I trading profitably?

A well thought out computerised accounts installation will tell you this, and more besides. We have seen that computerised accounting programs contain reporting routines which provide worthwhile and valuable information with no effort. Of course, you are not confined to the reporting routines available within the accounts program. You can 'export' accounts data to other programs where it can be manipulated and presented in a wide variety of ways. This is the subject of the next chapter.

Let the computer do the hard work

Chapter 9

Working with Other Computer Packages

The accounts software is a major source of valuable information. This data is too valuable to be confined just to the accounts department. The data can be used to help other departments like:

- the sales people with past sales statistics
- the production people with material and labour costs
- the stores people with stock data
- the estimators with current costs and trends
- the administration staff with overhead information etc.

All of these people can be provided with reports generated from within the accounts program. However, we can go one stage further. We can actually *give* them accounts information and let them play with it in any way that they choose. Normally the data will be manipulated in a spreadsheet, wordprocessor or database program. This process of exporting data works because other departments can manipulate data without the risk of corrupting the accounts information, as would happen if they had direct access to the accounts computer.

In fact, Microsoft have devised a special routine which enables data to be 'exported' from accounting packages to Word, Excel, Access and Miscrosoft Visual Basic. This system is called 'Open Data Base Connectivity' or ODBC for short. Once you have installed your ODBC driver in your accounts package, you can read your accounts data directly from other applications. The ODBC driver is 'read only' so you cannot write data back into the accounts program. This prevents the accounts data from accidental corruption. Some versions of Sage include an ODBC driver.

For the purpose of illustration, let us have a look at what a spreadsheet can do. Here are a few notes for people who may be new to spreadsheets.

Spreadsheets

Many people have been introduced to the use of computers through spreadsheets like Lotus 123, Excel and SuperCalc. Arguably, it was the availability of Visicalc on the very early Apple machines which made personal computing take off in the first place. You can do all sorts of calculations using a spreadsheet package.

What is a Spreadsheet Package?

A spreadsheet is an arrangement of rows and columns to form a grid (see example on page 90). The columns run from left to right across the spreadsheet and are usually labelled with a letter starting at A, running through to Z, then AA, AB, AC etc. Most spreadsheets have at least 256 columns which takes you up to Column HP. Rows run from top to bottom down the spreadsheet and are numbered sequentially (1, 2, 3 etc), often going to 16,000 rows or even beyond.

Where a row and a column intersect, they form a 'cell'. Each cell can be referenced by the co-ordinates of its column letter and row number. For example, a spreadsheet going to column HP and row 8,192 would have 2,097,152 cells in the spreadsheet.

Your spreadsheet can produce graphs!

Data can be entered into the spreadsheet in the form of text, numbers and formulae. Formulae can consist of:

- – numbers
- – mathematical operations (eg add, subtract, multiply, divide etc)
- – cell references.

Thus the formula '1+1' may be inputed giving the answer '2'. Or, you can tell the spreadsheet to add the contents of cell 'A1' to the contents of cell 'A2' and to put the result in cell 'A3'. A comprehensive range of mathematical, statistical and logical functions are available, if required.

A spreadsheet package is powerful because it can manipulate data. It is possible to:

- • copy and move cells and blocks of cells within the spreadsheet
- • insert or delete rows and columns
- • erase the contents of cells
- • carry out 'what if' analysis by substituting different values
- • sort and rearrange data
- • print out the result as hard copy or save it as a file for later retrieval
- • build in links between different spreadsheets.

Here are a few tips for working with spreadsheets.

Planning

Spreadsheets like any other project need planning

> *'If we don't know where we're going, we'll end up some place else!'*
> Sir John Harvey-Jones

Ask yourself the following questions:

- – What is the purpose of the spreadsheet?
- – Who is it for?
- – What message is the spreadsheet supposed to convey?
- – Will the user (not the creator) be able to understand the output?

Design

Build the spreadsheet up in stages – we recommend the diamond formation illustrated below. This ensures that new rows and columns can be added without affecting other sections.

	Sales							
			Purchases					
					Cashbook			

If you have common entries which will be used in different places in the spreadsheet, lay them all out in a similar way. This enables you to use the 'copy' command to maximum effect.

Lay information out neatly in columns and rows in such a way that you can use the 'sum' formula rather than having to add lots of individual cells together.

Label column and row headings so that you know what the figures are supposed to represent.

Take great care over the 'output' part of the spreadsheet, even if this means duplicating information in the spreadsheet – the output is the most important aspect.

Avoid

- Overcomplicated formulae – virtually impossible to debug. Build them up in stages.

- Incomprehensible output.

- Lotus 123 syndrome – the desire to produce page after page of neatly printed listing paper covered in figures which no-one can possibly take in.

Lotus 123 syndrome?

	A	B	C	D	E	F	G	H	I	J	K	L
1	Spreadsheet Example for a Garden Centre											
2												
3		ACTUAL		ACTUAL		BUDGET		BY MONTH				
4		YEAR TO		YEAR TO		YEAR		MAY	JUNE	JULY	AUG	SEPT
5		30.04.95		30.04.96		30.04.97						
6		£	%	£	%	£	%					
7	SALES											
8	Department											
9	1 PLANTS & SHRUBS	70000	39	85000	39	100000	39	20000	25000			
10	2 GARDEN FURNITURE	18000	10	22000	10	25000	9	5000	5000			
11	3 COMPOSTS	20000	11	23000	10	30000	11	5000	5000			
12	4 FERTILISERS	40000	22	50000	23	60000	23	10000	8000			
13	5 OTHER SALES	30000	17	40000	18	50000	18	4000	4000			
14	TOTAL SALES	178000	100	220000	100	265000	100	44000	47000			
15												
16	COST OF SALES											
17	Department											
18	1 PLANTS & SHRUBS	50000	71	59500	70	70000	70	14000	17500			
19	2 GARDEN FURNITURE	9000	50	11000	50	12500	50	2500	2500			
20	3 COMPOSTS	11000	55	12500	54	16800	56	2800	2800			
21	4 FERTILISERS	26000	65	32000	64	39600	66	6600	5280			
22	5 OTHER SALES	15000	50	20000	50	25000	50	2000	2000			
23	TOTAL COST OF SALES	111000	62	135000	61	163900	61	27900	30080			
24												
25	GROSS PROFIT											
26	Department											
27	1 PLANTS & SHRUBS	20000	29	25500	30	30000	30	6000	7500			
28	2 GARDEN FURNITURE	9000	50	11000	50	12500	50	2500	2500			
29	3 COMPOSTS	9000	45	10500	46	13200	44	2200	2200			
30	4 FERTILISERS	14000	35	18000	36	20400	34	3400	2720			
31	5 OTHER SALES	15000	50	20000	50	25000	50	2000	2000			
32												
33	TOTAL GROSS PROFIT	67000	38	85000	39	101100	38	16100	16920			

Excel Pivot Tables

If you are an experienced Excel user, why not develop the spreadsheet idea a little further? You may find that your accounts software includes an ODBC driver. This can be used to read data directly into an Excel pivot table. A pivot table is a powerful way to compare and summarise data. If you want to change the way in which the data is sorted or displayed, you can create a whole new report simply by dragging and dropping fields to meet your revised needs. Some versions of Sage software come with Excel ODBC templates which you can use to generate reports in Excel.

Additional Software

Computer software houses are always ready to increase their sales by providing additional bolt-on modules. These additional modules work with the basic accounts software to provide additional functions. For example, Sage will also supply:

- payroll software
- self assessment software
- customer contact management software
- time and fee billing software
- on-line banking software.

All of these additional products can be used to boost the power of your basic accounting system.

Summary

With all the tools at your disposal, you should be able to control:

- the *type* of information available
- the *quality* of the information available
- the *timelines* of the information
- the *control* you have over that information
- the way the information helps you *manage* the business.

Filing Your Records

Even though we live in the age of electronic mail, the Internet and the worldwide web, it is surprising how much paperwork you have to handle. You still have to keep copies of invoices, receipts, bills etc because they may be required during a VAT inspection. Similarly, your auditor will want to see a sample of your invoices to satisfy himself that the accounts are in order. A lack of paperwork could also get you into big trouble with the Inland Revenue if you suffer a tax investigation. In this case, you will need every bit of evidence you can muster! For these reasons, you have to support your computerised accounting records with paper files. Here are some suggestions on how to maintain your files.

Sales Invoice File

If you sell items on credit, you must keep a copy of
each sales invoice sent to customers.

These can be kept in an ordinary ring binder. Punch
two holes in the duplicate copy of the sales invoice
and put it into the 'Unpaid Sales Invoices' ring binder.
Do this immediately after it is printed. Avoid the
temptation to file the invoices at a later date. If the
invoices are filed immediately, they cannot get lost.

Remember to number each invoice sequentially. If you destroy any invoices, keep a
copy to prove that you haven't sold something without showing the proceeds in your
accounts. Clearly describe the goods despatched or the service performed and show
the VAT you have added. Some customers use an incomplete invoice as a reason for
delaying payment.

When an invoice is paid, transfer it to another ring
binder clearly labelled 'Paid Sales Invoices'. Write the
date and number of the cheque you receive on the
invoice.

By using this simple system, no invoice should get lost
because it will be filed immediately it is printed. All
unpaid invoices come quickly to hand because they
are in date order. File *'paid'* sales invoices in invoice
number order. This will make it easy to trace old
invoices should it be necessary.

If you only receive part payment of an invoice, write on the invoice the amount you
have received but *do not* transfer it into the 'paid' file until it has been fully paid.

Purchase Invoice File

File your purchase invoices as soon as they are received in an 'Unpaid Purchase Invoices' file. This ensures that the invoice cannot get lost. To help find invoices in the future, allocate a serial reference number of your own. This can be written on the invoice in red ink. Special stamping machines are available if you have to label large numbers of purchase invoices. Keep delivery notes and credit notes in the same file. Attach them to the invoice when it is sent to you.

When the invoice is paid, transfer it to a 'Paid Purchase Invoices' file. This means that you can always check up on how much is owed and to whom. When you pay an invoice, write your cheque number on the invoice. This provides an important link between your banking records and your purchase records.

If only part payment of an invoice is made, write on the invoice the amount you have paid but *do not* transfer it into the 'paid' file until it has been fully paid.

Banking Records

It is important to keep track of your bank position. Ask your bank to send you a monthly statement. Statements can be kept in a ring binder or one of the special folders issued by the bank.

Now that banks do not return used cheques, it is important that you fill in cheque counterfoils and retain them. They should be filed in an envelope or special (small) drawer as they are easily lost. Cheque stubs may be your best link between an amount paid by cheque and the goods/services to which they relate. Enter the supplier's invoice number and any reference number you may devise, as well as the name, date etc on the counterfoil.

Keep your bank paying-in book to hand. This will enable you to check that cheques have been entered correctly into your account.

Petty Cash

In order to save your cash account from unnecessary clutter, many people operate a Petty Cash Book. This book contains details of very small amounts of money spent. Totals from the petty cash book are periodically transferred to the accounts program when there are sufficient entries to make this worthwhile.

The 'imprest' system is an attractive way of controlling petty cash. A certain sum of money, say £100, is chosen as the imprest amount. This sum is selected because it is enough to meet the petty cash needs for a period of, say, a week or month. The money is put into a tin or other receptacle. As money is spent, the corresponding receipts are put into the imprest tin. The sum of the receipts, plus cash, must always add back to the original imprest amount. When cash gets low, the imprest is topped up by exchanging the receipts for more cash.

This simple system has the following advantages:

- There is an upper limit to the amount of money which can be kept in the petty cash tin at any one time. This minimises the impact of theft.

- Theft can be detected easily since the sum of receipts plus cash will not add back to the imprest amount.

- The number of entries in the accounts are reduced to a minimum. An entry is only made when there is an imprest 'top-up'.

- Petty cash can be collected together and accounted for in one place by one person.

If you travel a lot and have few petty cash items, you may prefer to use an ordinary desk diary as your petty cash record. This has space for each day of the year into which you can record the amount of money spent. If working away from base, the desk diary can be taken with you so that no items will be forgotten while you are away.

Receipts for Cash Spent by You

It is important to keep all cash receipts because:

- they form part of your records
- they are evidence of your purchase in the event of a dispute with your supplier
- they may be requested by the VAT inspector
- they could, possibly, be required by the income tax inspector.

Again, a simple ring binder should be sufficient for your needs. According to the number and type of receipts, you may decide to classify them by type of purchase, otherwise date order should suffice. Small receipts can be stapled to a page and labelled with type or date of purchase.

Record of Cash Received

You will need some record of cash received. If you have a lot of cash receipts, you will probably install a till so that amounts are automatically recorded. If you have a few cash receipts, you will only keep a record of daily totals.

Chapter 11

Entering Data and Correcting Mistakes

Most computerised acccounting packages maintain their records in double entry format. This can be quite confusing to the majority of people who aren't experts in double entry book-keeping methods.

Most of the time the package shields the operator from the mechanics of double entry. For example, if you are raising a sales invoice, the computer will automatically:

- debit the customer's account with the VAT *inclusive* value of the invoice
- credit the sales account with the VAT *exclusive* value of the invoice
- credit the VAT account with the VAT charged to the customer.

By the same token, the computer is programmed to make the double entry transactions automatically for:

- purchase invoices entered
- purchase payments made
- sales invoices raised
- sales receipts collected
- bank transfers.

Double entry

Indeed, if you only make routine entries then you may not even be aware that the transactions are being recorded in double entry format. Eventually, however, you will have to make a correction or enter a journal using double entry principles. These notes have been written to help anyone who hasn't had much contact with double entry to far.

Double Entry Book-keeping

Most small businesses record their transactions in an analysed cashbook. Once the business outgrows the cashbook, it will graduate to a computerised accounting system. This means that many book-keepers have no experience of manual double entry book-keeping. It is not surprising, therefore, that these book-keepers get their first taste of double entry when things start to go wrong with the computerised accounting system.

As the name suggests, double entry involves recording each transaction twice. One entry is made in the account *receiving* the value. The other entry is made in the account *giving* the value. For example, if you bought stock for cash, one entry would reflect the cash leaving the cash account. The other entry would reflect the stock entering the stock account. There are a few rules concerning double entry.

- Entries are always made in one of two columns. The left-hand column is called the debit entry, the right-hand column is called the credit entry.

- Every time an entry is made on the credit side of one account, an equal amount must be entered on the debit side of another account.

- Each entry should show the date and description of the transaction.

- Accounts are broken down into three categories. These are:
  - asset accounts
  - liability accounts
  - capital accounts.

Each of these accounts has its own rules which determine whether an entry is a debit entry or a credit entry. Here are the rules for each type of account.

Asset Accounts

An asset is something owned by the business which has a value. For example, bank, stock, cash, debtors, vehicles, plant and equipment, buildings etc are all assets. To *increase* the value in an asset account, enter the value on the *debit* (or left-hand) side. To *decrease* the value in an asset account, enter the value on the *credit* or (right-hand) side. The total value contained in the account is the sum of all the debit entries less the sum of all the credit entries.

Any Asset Account

Debit	Credit
Increases	Decreases
+	−

For example, if you bought a van for £6,000 with a cheque, your entries would look as follows:

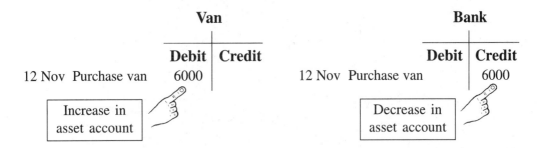

	Van				**Bank**	
	Debit	**Credit**			**Debit**	**Credit**
12 Nov Purchase van	6000			12 Nov Purchase van		6000

Increase in asset account

Decrease in asset account

You are probably thinking that these entries must be wrong! How can the entry in the bank account be a credit? Everyone knows that a credit is an increase in the bank account. We are showing it as a decrease. What has gone wrong? The answer is simple. Most people's perception of bank debits and credits is based on the bank statement but the bank statement is not a record of *your* account with the bank. It is a record of the bank's account with *you*. This means that the bank's entries are the opposite way round to the entries in your own books. If you remember that money entering your bank account is a debit, you won't go far wrong.

Liability Accounts

A liability is an amount which your business is 'liable' to pay sometime. For example, trade creditors and loans are liabilities because you will have to be paid sooner or later.

To *increase* the value in a liability account, enter the value on the *credit* side. To *decrease* the value in a liability account, enter the value on the *debit* side.

These entries are, of course, the opposite to the entries in the asset account.

Any Liability Account

Debit	Credit
Decreases	Increases
−	+

Here is an example. Suppose you buy £2,000 of stock on credit. Here are the transactions.

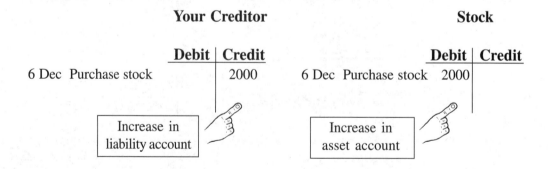

Your Creditor			Stock		
	Debit	Credit		Debit	Credit
6 Dec Purchase stock		2000	6 Dec Purchase stock	2000	

Increase in liability account

Increase in asset account

Notice that we have increased the amount in the creditor's account by crediting it. We now need an equal and opposite debit entry. This comprises £2,000 added to the stock account. We increase the value of in asset account by debiting it.

The Capital Account

Capital is money put into the firm by the owners. It behaves like a liability account. The double entry for capital accounts is the same as for any other liability account.

The Capital Account

Debit	Credit
Decreases	Increases
–	+

Here is an example. An investor purchases £1,500 worth of shares in the business. You put the money into the bank.

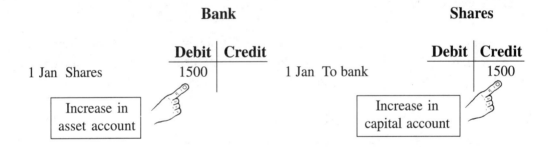

Bank

	Debit	Credit
1 Jan Shares	1500	

Increase in asset account

Shares

	Debit	Credit
1 Jan To bank		1500

Increase in capital account

Some Simple Rules of Thumb

It can sometimes be difficult to work out whether an item should be a debit or a credit. You can work it out from the rules we have just explained or you can use the following rough and ready guide if you get stuck.

- Money moving into your bank account is always a debit.

- Business expenses such as rent, rates, heat, light, electric etc are debits (because you pay them off with a credit entry at the bank).

- The two most common credit entries are 'Capital Introduced' and 'Sales'. The corresponding debits result in cash moving into the bank account.

Value Added Tax

VAT represents an unwelcome complication to double entry transactions. Registered traders collect VAT from their customers on behalf of HM Customs and Excise. Periodically, the VAT that has been collected is paid to Customs & Excise.

VAT that has been collected on a sale becomes a *credit* on the VAT account. If it helps, you can think of VAT collected as an increase in VAT *liable* to be paid at a later date. An increase in a liability account is, of course, a credit. VAT that is paid over to HM Customs and Excise is a debit to the VAT account since this payment decreases the VAT liability.

VAT which is paid out on purchases reduces the VAT liable to be paid to Customs and Excise since it offsets VAT collected on sales. This means that VAT paid out on purchases is a debit on the VAT account since it decreases the amount of VAT liable to be paid to HMC&E.

One of the great benefits of computerised accounting is that it handles VAT on sales and purchases without the operator really being involved. This is great until something goes wrong. It then becomes necessary to 'unwind' a mistake involving VAT.

Double Entry Examples – Sales

Here are some double entry examples including VAT, they use a VAT rate of 17½%.

Cash Sale

Sell goods to the value of £100 + VAT for cash.

Cash		Sales		VAT	
Dr	Cr	Dr	Cr	Dr	Cr
117.50			100.00		17.50

Credit Sale

Sell goods to the value of £200 + VAT on credit to Jones.

Jones		Sales		VAT	
Dr	Cr	Dr	Cr	Dr	Cr
235.00			200.00		35.00

Jones pays for his goods.

Bank		Jones	
Dr	Cr	Dr	Cr
235.00		235.00	235.00

Goods Returned

Jones returns £60 of goods (£70.50 including VAT). We give him a refund. Entries are:

Bank		Jones		Sales		VAT	
Dr	Cr	Dr	Cr	Dr	Cr	Dr	Cr
235.00		235.00	235.00		200.00		35.00
	70.50	70.50	70.50	60.00		10.50	

Double Entry Examples – Purchases

Here are some double entry examples including VAT at the rate of 17½%.

Cash Purchase

Buy goods to the value of £100 + VAT for cash.

Cash			Purchases			VAT	
Dr	**Cr**		**Dr**	**Cr**		**Dr**	**Cr**
	117.50		100.00			17.50	

Credit Transaction

Car repairs costing £94 including VAT on credit.

Garage			Car Repairs			VAT	
Dr	**Cr**		**Dr**	**Cr**		**Dr**	**Cr**
	94.00		80.00			14.00	

Pay garage.

Bank			Garage	
Dr	**Cr**		**Dr**	**Cr**
	94.00			94.00
			94.00	

Refunds

If the garage gave us a refund of £10 ex VAT (£11.50 including VAT), entries are:

Bank			Garage			Car Repairs			VAT	
Dr	**Cr**		**Dr**	**Cr**		**Dr**	**Cr**		**Dr**	**Cr**
	94.00			94.00		80.00			14.00	
11.75			94.00				10.00			1.75
			11.75	11.75						

Double Entry Exercise (including effects of VAT)

Complete the double entries for the following transactions:

1   12 May   Cash sale for £94 including VAT
2   16 May   Cash sale for £60 excluding VAT
3   20 May   Credit sale to Smith for £600 excluding VAT
4   21 May   Refund to Smith for £141 including VAT
5   26 May   Smith pays his debt
6   29 May   Credit sales to Evans for £352.50 including VAT

	Bank			**Sales**	
	Dr	Cr		Dr	Cr

	Bank			**Sales**	
	Dr	Cr		Dr	Cr

	Bank			**Sales**	
	Dr	Cr		Dr	Cr

Check your answer with the model in Appendix 1.

Correcting Errors in Accounts Software

There are two ways to correct errors. These are:

- Use the in-built error correction routines.
- Amend the errors using journal debits and journal credits.

Here is a little more detail.

In-built Correction Routines

This is the safest method to use if you do not feel confident with double entry. From the main menu, select 'Maintenance'.

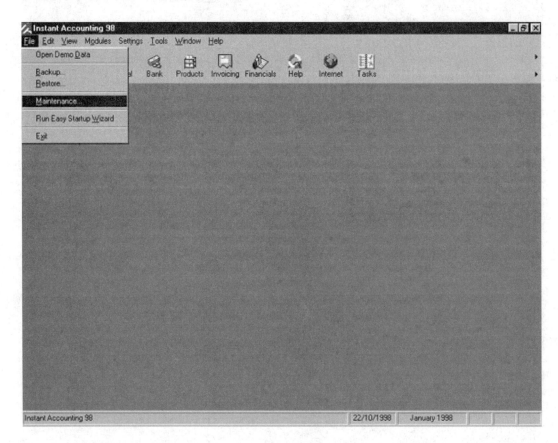

From the 'File Maintenance' menu, select 'Corrections' which is the bottom box on the left.

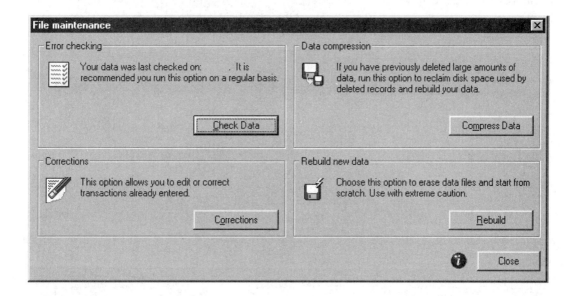

Once you have selected Corrections, you will see a Posting Error Correction screen along the lines of the one shown below.

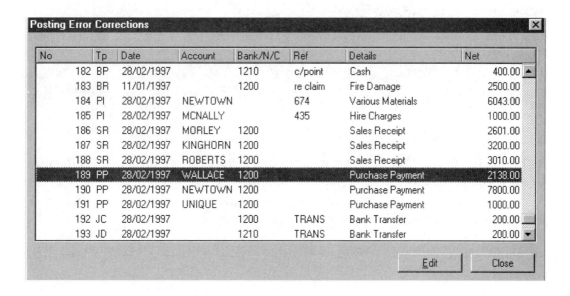

The Posting Error Corrections screen shows all the transactions entered onto the computer so far this financial year. You can select a transaction by highlighting that transaction followed by pressing the 'Edit' button. This will reveal the Edit Transaction Header Record screen as shown below.

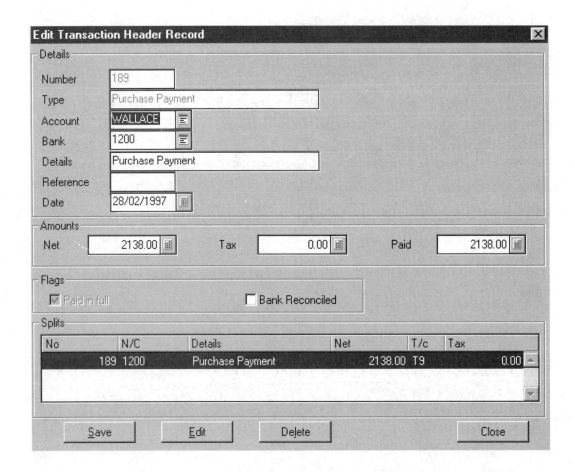

At this point, you can either edit the entry or delete it. If you are unsure, it is probably better to delete the entry and re-enter the data from scratch. The edit button allows you to edit most of the fields contained in the record. Once you are happy with your edit changes, press 'Save' to record your amendments.

Corrections Using Journal Entries

If you feel confident with double entry, you can amend your records by placing journal debit and journal credit entries into your records. Traditionally, mistakes in double entry systems were rectified by placing an equal and opposite debit or credit entry into the account you want to amend, this cancels the old entry. You then insert the correct entry into the account.

This is how to make journal corrections. From the main menu, select the 'Nominal' icon. From the Nominal menu, select 'Journals'. You will be presented with the screen shown below.

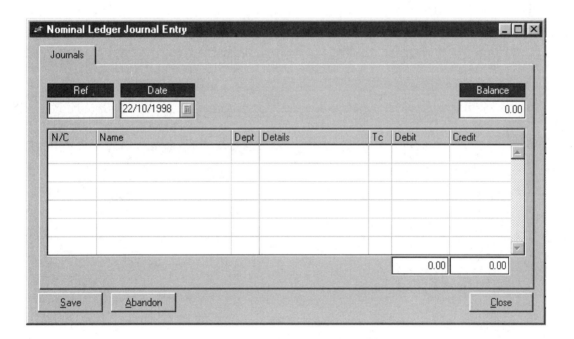

You now need to work out the double entries which would have been involved in making the original (erroneous) transaction. Don't forget to include the effects of VAT if the transaction was a VATable one.

You now enter equal and opposite entries onto the lines of the journal entry screen. The program will not let you save the results unless your entries balance. This is shown when the 'balance' box towards the top right of the screen registers zero.

You can use the Nominal Ledger Journal Entry screen for all sorts of adjustments. In addition to error corrections, you can use it to enter accruals, prepayments and depreciation.

Chapter 12

Preventing Fraud

The person responsible for the accounting system inevitable assumes some responsibility for stewardship of the business assets. Put bluntly, this means that the accounts manager ought to be on the lookout for fraud.

There is evidence to suggest that most fraud is committed by staff rather than outsiders. Indeed, some fraudsters are senior level employees who have betrayed the trust placed in them.

Fraud is tempting because many executives have only a skimpy knowledge of computers and an even skinnier knowledge of accounting. Few attempts are made to detect fraud. Frauds that are detected are often hushed up. It is probably easier to defraud a company with a computerised accounting system than a manual one. This is because Management leaves the computerised accounting system well alone on the basis that it is best left to people who understand that sort of thing. This is a great scenario for the fraudster.

As far as fraud prevention goes, there is little difference between a computerised system and a manual one. Both systems rely on the same routines and controls to ensure that everything is in order.

Fraud can be perpetuated by people inside, or outside, the company. It can involve the theft of money, goods or time. We have broken fraud down into two accounting areas. These are frauds affecting the main accounting system and fraud affecting the payroll system. We have included payroll because it is a particularly tempting area for fraudsters. In many companies, wages is the biggest single item of expenditure.

Here are some of the steps you can take to minimise fraud.

Payroll Fraud

There are many ways in which employees can fraudulently get money (or favours) from the payroll system. Here are some of them.

- Create a dummy employee. A real employee draws the wage for the dummy employee.

- Continue to pay an employee who has left. The fraudster collects the employee's wage.

- Pay non existent casual workers. This is a particularly tempting fraud when the pay is below the PAYE and NI thresholds.

- Pay overtime or bonus payments to individuals who have not earned them. Split the proceeds with the individual concerned.

- Give holiday pay to individuals in excess of that allowed in the Contract of Employment. Secure some form of favour by way of return.

- Create a fictitious foreign employee or consultant. This is particularly attractive since payments are remitted abroad with no deductions of PAYE and NI. The UK tax authorities are unlikely to audit these wage payments.

- Arrange to make inflated payments to casual staff/subcontractors/associates who then give back part of the payment to the individual perpetrating the fraud.

- Pay expenses and benefits to individuals who are not entitled to receive them, possibly in return for cash or 'favours'.

- Unscrupulous *employers* have been known to retain PAYE and NI payments instead of paying the tax to the Inland Revenue. This can create difficulties for employees attempting to claim unemployment benefits if the company, subsequently, becomes insolvent.

- Unscrupulous employers have been known to create dummy pension schemes. Employees' pension contributions are then misappropriated.

- Check for differences between the amounts calculated on the P11s and the amounts shown on the payslips. It is possible to misappropriate part of an employee's wage if the employee can't be bothered to check his deductions (or wasn't given enough detail to do so).

- An individual in the payroll office could misappropriate the proceeds of a Payroll Giving scheme or Save As You Earn scheme.

- Although Electronic Fund Transfer is an inherently safe way of transferring money, a miscreant with access to the code words could transfer money illegally. There should be a limit on the maximum amount that can be made via EFT on any individual's wage payment.

- No employee should be responsible for calculating wage payments *and* signing cheques. There must be an independent authorisation to make payments, irrespective of how the payment is made.

- Some sample wage payments should be checked periodically from start to finish. This systematic approach could highlight problems which might not be discovered by occasional random checks.

Payroll fraud!

Accounts Based Fraud

Supplier Fraud

Be careful that you do not pay for goods which have:

- never been ordered
- are short of the delivery quantity required
- are not of the quality required.

Purchases should be raised on a properly authorised purchase order which stipulates price, quality, quantity and delivery date. The purchase order should be signed off by the manager whose budget will, eventually, bear the cost. Once delivered, the goods should be checked against the original purchase order to ensure that the delivery complies with that original order. Once delivery has been approved, the delivery note can be passed to the accounts department ready for payment. Supplier fraud is neither easier nor harder with a computerised accounting system. However, good accounts software makes it administratively easier to operate budgets, purchase orders and payments.

Fraud Involving Cash

Cash is a tempting target for theft, in areas like retail business, you can't avoid it. In shops, it is essential to put all cash transactions through the till. Insist that each customer is given a receipt. Clear the till and bank the proceeds intact on a regular basis, at least once a day. Keep the till rolls. It is important that your till rolls cross relate to your bankings for several reasons. First it convinces *you* that money which has been entered into the till has been banked. Secondly, it convinces the VAT man, auditor and Inland Revenue that you are honest. Under-recording of takings is probably the most common form of tax fraud. Your various inspectors and auditors will check whether you do it.

Make sure that nobody is allowed to take money from the till to pay for petty cash items. Insist that all petty cash items are paid for out of a separate petty cash box. This box should be maintained under the Imprest system which was explained earlier in the book.

Periodically, work out whether your cash receipts are what you would expect, bearing in mind your opening and closing stock and purchases for the sales period. From your knowledge of stock, purchases and gross margin, check how much of your 'purchases' works its way through to 'sales'. Be particularly careful if you sell attractive items like cigarettes, drink and other luxury items, they may disappear before they even reach the till!

If you bank *all* of your cash receipts regularly, you shouldn't have much cash in hand. If you have to keep cash in hand, reconcile your computer cash balance with the physical cash in hand regularly.

For those businesses which don't have to deal with cash from sales, the easiest solution is to hold only petty cash. All payments should be made via the bank using cheques, BACS and direct debits. With luck, you may be able to control cash by simply not having it lying around the business!

Bank Reconciliation

Not all money that goes missing disappears by fraud. Some money disappears by mistake. The bank is one area where these mistakes can happen. Make sure that money doesn't leak via the bank account by reconciling your bank balance with your computerised accounting records at least once a month. For reasons of genuine mistake, you could find that your bank account is not credited with money that you have earned. Alternatively, money could have been paid out of your bank account in error.

Company Credit Cards

You may issue business credit cards to individuals to enable them to purchase petrol, meals, hotel bills etc without dipping into their own personal resources. It goes without saying that all credit card statements need to be checked against receipts because of the temptation to bill personal items on to a company credit card. You may find items like entertaining, petrol for private vehicles, furniture and household goods appearing on the credit card statement. These purchases will give you big problems with the VAT man and Inland Revenue for tax avoidance reasons. No matter how senior the individual, buying personal items on the business should be avoided. It creates problems with both business accounting records and tax records.

Fraud by Electronic Commerce

In the good old days, staff were more likely to take money by stealing cash or having cheques made out to people who shouldn't receive it. Today, however, there is an increasing trend towards the use of Electronic Funds Transfer (EFT). It is now routine for businesses to pay their employees by EFT. Many businesses settle their invoices using the Banking Automated Clearing System (BACS) and the Internet now offers options for payment via debit and credit cards. Although the basic fraud problem hasn't changed, each level of increased sophistication leaves a few more managers unable to cope with the complexities of technical change. Irrespective of how money changes hands, all payments should be authorised by a responsible individual. In theory, electronic fund transfer should make the checking of transactions easier not harder. Be careful that the passwords used for EFT do not become common knowledge. Also ensure that there is a ceiling on the amount of money that can be transferred in this way. It would be pretty galling if the clerk who normally transfers £200 by EFT decides to transfer £500,000 to another bank account, especially if it is based in Rio de Janeiro!

Control of Customers

Ninety nine per cent of customers are worthy, honest individuals who pay their bills with no trouble at all. However, a small per cent will order goods for which they are either unable, or unwilling, to pay. These people drain the business of cash through bad debt. Ensure that customers who are offered the privilege of credit do not abuse that privilege. You need some system for checking credit, especially if the sums involved are large. The subject is too big to cover in this book; however, it is covered in another book in the series called *Simple and Practical Costing, Pricing and Credit Control.*

Credit control is not an exciting job. It is hard to get enthusiastic about chasing customers for money. Even if customers eventually pay up, slow payers can leave substantial amounts of cash in their hands instead of in your business bank account. Computerised accounting has made the mechanics of credit control much easier. However, you still need the human effort to chase customers for payment. A good credit control system will keep the lid on bad and doubtful debts.

Computers help you to get your money in

Chapter 13

Computerised Accounting Tutorial

In this tutorial we will use the copy of *Instant Accounting* which can be found attached to the inside back cover of this book.

Install *Instant Accounting* according to the instructions in Chapter 3. Load the program and open the File menu as shown below. The top option in the File menu will either be 'Open Instant Data' or 'Open Demo Data'. Click the top option (if neccessary) to read 'Open Instant Data'.

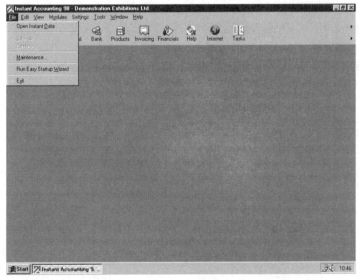

Before we can enter accounts data in our exercise, we need to set up the program. This includes inputting:

- Company information

- Customer information
- Supplier information.

We also need to choose a Chart of Accounts.

The Exercise

We will set up the program, starting with company information.

Company Information

From the File menu, select 'Run Easy Startup Wizard'. We will now input the business:

- name
- telephone number
- VAT registration number
- financial year start date
- select the standard VAT scheme.

Select the Easy Startup Wizard from the File menu shown on the previous page. The Easy Startup Wizard presents you with a number of introductory screens. Page through these screens using the 'Next' button, noting the contents as you go, until you reach the Name and Address screen shown below. Complete the screen as shown.

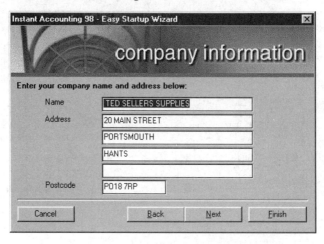

Select 'Next' to move onto the Company Contact Numbers screen. Complete the screen as shown below.

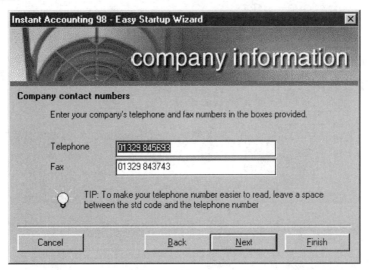

Select 'Next' to move on to the VAT registration screen. Ted Sellers is VAT registered so we need to complete the screen as follows.

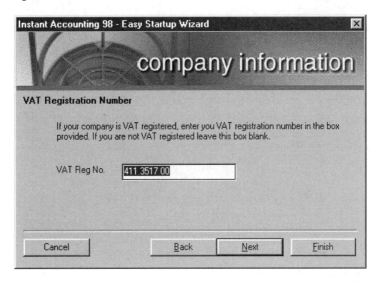

Press the 'Next' button which will reveal the Financial Year Start Date screen as shown overleaf. Our exercise starts on 1 January 1998 so it is important for you to complete the screen as shown.

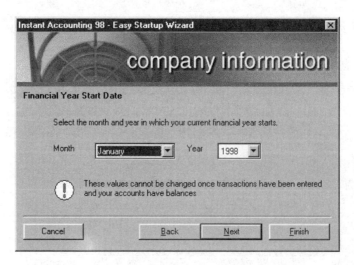

You will be asked to confirm the financial year start date which you do by pressing 'Next'.

You will next be asked to complete the VAT registration scheme. Ted Sellers accounts for VAT under the Standard VAT Scheme. Complete the screen as follows.

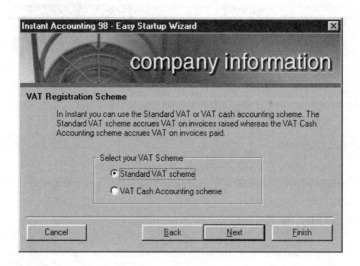

Use the 'Next' button to move onto 'Setup Company Departments' screen. In this exercise, we will not be using company departments so press the 'Next' button and select 'No' when asked if you want to set up departmental analysis. This completes the company set up. The following screens deal with customer information.

Customer Information

Press the 'Next' button until you reach the following screen requesting customer information.

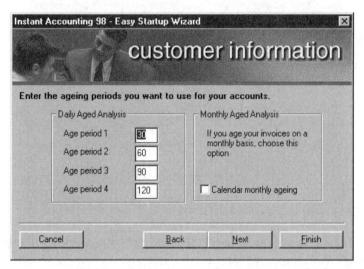

In our case, we will accept the default ageing periods for customer debt reporting which are shown in increments of 30 days.

If you select the 'Next' button, you will be presented with the following screen. Enter the credit limit and settlement terms as shown.

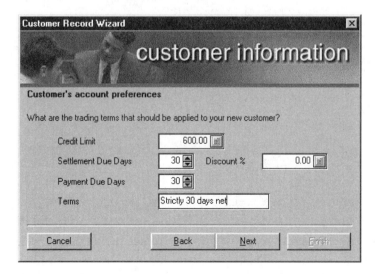

Press 'Next' to reveal the screen shown below. This tells the accounts program which nominal account it should use to store the sales figures for the business. Accept this default.

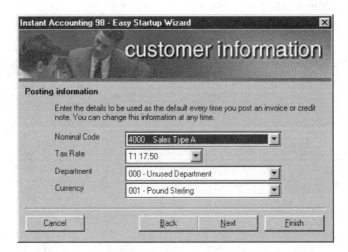

This completes the customer information section. Pressing 'Next' will take you into the Supplier Information section.

Supplier Information

Press 'Next' until you reach the following screen.

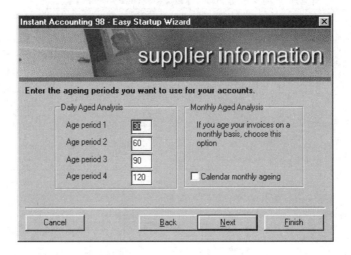

This screen allows you to set boundaries around your aged creditor report. Accept the defaults and proceed to the next screen as shown below. Complete the screen as shown.

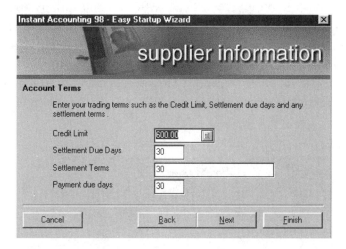

Continue to the next screen which sets the VAT rate applicable to purchases. It also determines the nominal code and currency for purchases. Since we are using the Sage default chart of accounts, the nominal code for materials purchased will be code 5000. Complete the screen as follows.

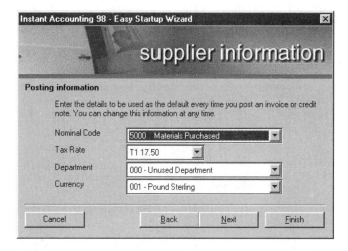

If you continue to press 'Next', you will eventually be asked if you want to analyse your stock into categories. For the purpose of this exercise, the answer is 'No'. Press the 'No' button and continue through products information.

Products Information

The first products information screen deals with decimal precision. You see many invoices where items which can only be billed in whole units are shown with two decimal points in the quantity field. This looks rather silly. In the case of Ted Sellers Supplies, all of Ted's products are billed in whole units so we will show them with zero decimal places, ie no decimal points. However, Ted's prices can be expressed in pennies so we need prices expressed to two decimal places. Complete the screen as follows.

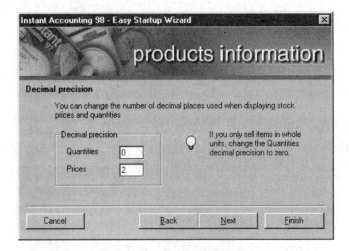

Press 'Next' to reveal the following screen.

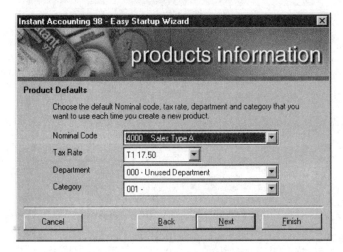

Notice that sales of Ted Seller's Products are stored in nominal code 4000. This is a repeat of information which we already entered earlier. We don't need to change anything so press 'Next' to complete the Products Information screens.

If you continue to press 'Next', you will enter the part of Startup Wizard which deals with task information. We will not set up task information as part of this tutorial so press 'Finish' to return to the main menu.

Choosing a Chart of Accounts

Sage incorporates a range of ten suggested layouts for charts of accounts. These suggested layouts range from builders to charitable bodies. For our purposes, however, we will adopt the 'general business' standard chart of accounts. Select it as follows. From the 'File' menu, choose 'Maintenance'. From the 'Maintenance' menu, choose rebuild new data.

Beware. Do not rebuild your accounts if you have already set up your real life data. This option will destroy your business data. Only run this tutorial <u>before</u> creating your data properly.

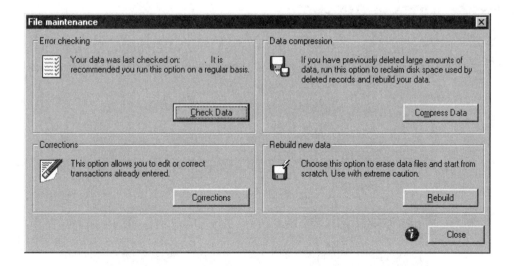

Select 'Rebuild'. [Rebuild] You will be presented with the Rebuild Data Files screen below.

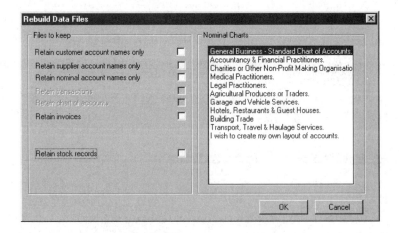

Adjust the boxes on the left side of the screen so that none of the boxes are ticked. Check that the screen looks like the screen shown above. Press 'OK'. The program will ask if you really do want to rebuild your accounts. Answer 'Yes' and you will see a request to enter your date for the start of the financial year. We originally set this to 1 Jan 1998 so we can confirm that this is OK.

View the Chart of Accounts

You can now have a look at your chosen chart of accounts. Select 'Nominal' from the toolbar. The chart of accounts is displayed in the window shown below.

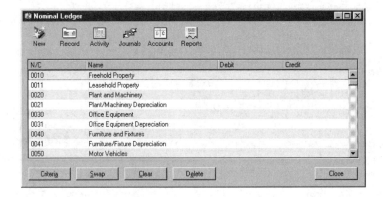

Scroll down the nominal account listing to see the names of the accounts available. We will only use a few of these accounts in this exercise. Before entering any data, we need to make a couple of adjustments to the 'standard' chart of accounts.

The default chart of accounts assumes that the trader is a company. Ted Sellers trades as a sole trader. In our example, this means that we have to change the 'standard' chart of accounts. Since sole traders don't issue shares, we need to change code 3000 from 'Ordinary Shares' into 'Capital'. We also need to delete code 3010 – Preferential Shares. Do this as follows.

- Highlight nominal code 3010 – Preferential Shares and press the 'Delete' button. You need to confirm your intention after which you will find that 'Preferential Shares' drops off the list.

Repeat the process for the following accounts, none of which relates to sole traders or partnerships.

3000 Ordinary Shares
7001 Directors Salaries
7002 Directors Renumeration

Use the 'New' wizard to create two new accounts. These are Capital and Drawings.

- Create a new nominal code for 'Capital' using code 3000 which we deleted earlier. Select the 'New' wizard. Type in the new nominal account name, ie 'Capital'. Then select the account type from the drop down list, ie Capital and Reserves. We have no nominal account opening balance to enter so select 'No', press 'Next' followed by 'Finish'. This will return you to the Nominal Ledger menu.

- Repeat the instructions above to create a 'Drawings' account (A/c no 3300). Drawings is money taken out of the business by the owner for his/her personal consumption.

Close the screen and follow the Ted Sellers instructions on the next page.

1 January Open business account with cheque for £350 drawn on personal bank account. The bank agrees to a £2000 overdraft facility.

What are We Trying to Do?

- Record the £350 cheque to open the business bank account. (A/c no 1200)

- Record the entry of £350 to the Capital Account. (A/c no 3000)

How Do We Do It?

Select 'Bank' from the main menu. Highlight '1200 Bank Current Account' from the Bank Accounts menu.

Select the 'Receipts' icon. You will be presented with the following screen.

Complete the screen as shown. Show the date as 1 Jan 1998. Press 'Save'. Close the Bank Receipts screen.

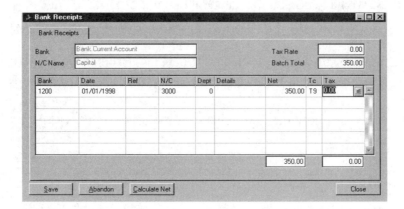

Did it Work?

 From the Bank Accounts Menu, select 'Record'. This shows you that the current bank account (A/c no 1200) has a balance of £350. Close the Bank Accounts screens and return to the main screen.

 Select 'Nominal' from the main menu. Select account number 3000 ie 'Capital' from the available nominal codes on display. Select 'Record'. Note that the account has a credit balance £350, which is fine. Close all menus.

Double Entry Transactions

		Bank Current A/c 1200				Capital A/c 3000	
		Dr	Cr			Dr	Cr
1 Jan	from Personal A/c	350.00		1 Jan	Bank A/c		350.00

8 January   Cheque drawn on business bank account for £50 petty cash.

What are We Trying to Do?

- Record the withdrawal of £50 cheque from the bank account.

- Record the receipt of £50 in Petty Cash.

How Do We Do It?

Select the 'Bank' icon from the main screen.

Highlight 'A/c 1200 Bank Current Account' from the Bank Accounts menu.

Select the 'Transfer' icon. You will be presented with the following screen. Complete it as shown. Use the 'Account Numbers' icon to choose the accounts you wish to transfer money between. Enter the amount i.e. £50 'Save', and close the Bank Transfer screen.

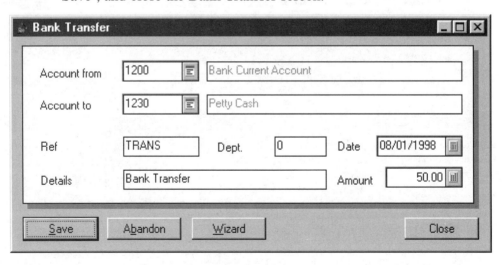

Did it Work?

Select A/c 1200 Bank Current Account from the Bank Accounts menu. Select 'Record'. Note that the bank now contains £300. This is shown as a debit balance. Close the bank record screen.

Select A/c 1230 Petty Cash from the Bank Accounts sub menu. Select 'Record'. Notice that the balance is £50.

Double Entry Transactions

		Bank Current A/c 1200				Petty Cash A/c 1230	
		Dr	Cr			Dr	Cr
1 Jan	from Personal A/c	350.00		8 Jan	from Bank A/c	50.00	
8 Jan	to Petty Cash		50.00				

8 January An invoice arrives for £44.65 incl VAT for business cards and letterheads from Smith's Printers, Newbold Street, Portsmouth, PO4 6XW. Enter the invoice and pay it off.

What are We Trying to Do?

- Record the stationery invoice on Smiths' Printers account.

- Record the expenditure on stationery in the stat nominal account.

- Record the payment of £44.65 by cheque from the bank.

- Clear Smith's Printers account.

- Update the VAT account.

How Do We Do It?

Before we can deal with any suppliers' transactions, we need to set up an account for them. To set up an account for Smith's Printers, proceed as follows.

Select 'Suppliers' from the main menu.

Select 'New' from the sub menu. Create Smith's account using the Suppliers Record Wizard. Complete the screens as shown.

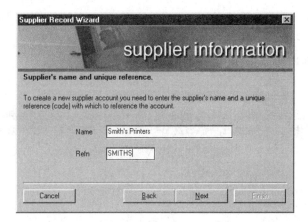

Enter the address on the next screen as follows.

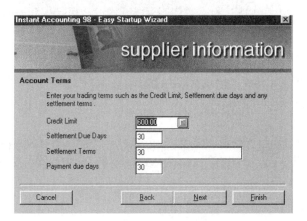

Press the 'next' button. Accept the values shown on the screen by pressing 'next..

You will now be presented with the screen shown below. We have never traded with Smith's Printer's before so we have no opening balance to put into the system. Complete the screen as shown. Press 'Next'.

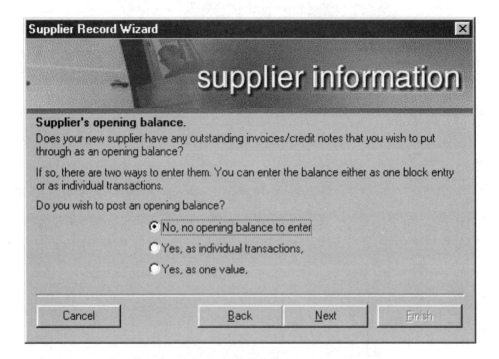

You have now completed the New Suppliers Wizard. Press 'Next' until you are offered a Finish button. Select 'Finish' and return to the main menu.

Entering Smith's Invoice and Paying the Amount

From the main menu select 'Suppliers'. From the Suppliers menu, select 'Invoices'. You will be presented with the following screen.

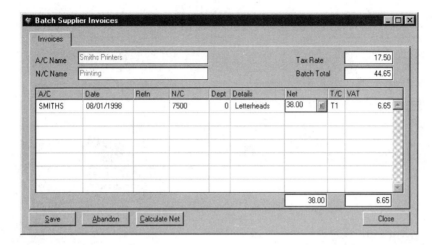

Complete the first line of the data entry. Select the small icon in the A/C column. Selecting this icon will present the name Smith's Printers. Highlight Smith's and select 'OK'. The abbreviation for Smith's Printers will appear in the Account column. Select the small icon to the right of the date field. Use the calendar to highlight the transaction date, which is 8 January 1998. We now need to charge the letterheads to the correct overhead account. If you check the default set of accounts, you will see that 'printing' is entered against nominal account code 7500. Click the cursor on the nominal code box and you will be presented with the Selection icon. If you click the icon, you will be presented with a sub menu of all nominal accounts available. Move the cursor down to code 7500 'Printing' and click 'OK'. Click on the details column and enter the description 'Letterheads'. The total amount paid to Smith's was £44.65 including VAT. If you enter £44.65 into the net column and click 'Calculate Net', the computer will automatically extract the VAT for you. When you are sure that the screen entries are correct, click 'Save', and return to the main menu.

Pay off Invoice

From the main menu select 'Bank'. From within Bank, select 'Suppliers'. You will be presented with the following screen.

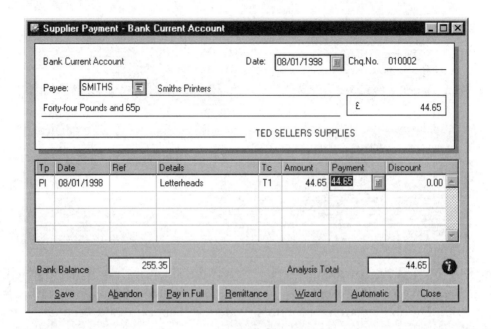

Complete the imitation cheque at the top of the screen. You will find that the payment details are automatically entered on the account on the lower half of the screen. Complete the payee, date and cheque number on the imitation cheque as shown. Then select 'Pay in Full' and 'Save'. The program will automatically pay off Smith's account. Close all screens.

Did it Work?

Check bank account:

From the main menu, select 'Bank'.

From the bank account, highlight Current Account A/c 1200. Then select 'Record'.

From Bank Record, select 'Activity'. Note the appearance of a credit for £44.65. Close Bank screens and return to the main menu.

Check Suppliers Account

From the main menu, select 'Suppliers'.

Highlight Smith's Account and press 'Activity'. Press 'OK' to the Activity Date Range screen. Note that the account now carries a zero balance, which is correct. Close all screens.

VAT Account

Note that these letterheads carried VAT which means that we should see a new VAT entry stemming from Smith's transaction.

From the main menu, select 'Nominal A/c'. From the 'Nominal Ledger', highlight the 'Purchase Tax Control Account'. (Account no 2201)

Select 'Activity', press 'OK' to accept the sub menu defaults. Note that the VAT related to the letterheads, ie £6.65 appears on the VAT account. Close the 'Purchase Tax Control Account'. Close all screens. Return to the main menu.

Check Printing Nominal A/c (No 7500)

From the main menu select 'Nominal Account'. Highlight the 'Printing Nominal Account No 7500'.

Select 'Activity' and accept the defaults. Note that the cost of the letterheads is shown excl VAT, ie £38.00.

Double Entry Transactions

Bank Current A/c 1200		
	Dr	Cr
1 Jan Open A/c	350.00	
8 Jan to Petty Cash		50.00
8 Jan to Smiths Printers		44.65

Smith's Printers A/c SMITHS		
	Dr	Cr
8 Jan L/heads		44.65
8 Jan from Bank	44.65	

VAT A/c 2200/1		
	Dr	Cr
8 Jan L/heads	6.65	

Printing A/c 7500		
	Dr	Cr
8 Jan L/heads	38.00	

9 January   Cheque drawn on business account for £99.88 to purchase stock comprising five widgits from N Sidwell & Sons. Widgets are to be resold to customers at a later date.

What Are We Trying to Do?

- Record the purchase invoice on Sidwell's account.

- Record the payment of £99.88 by cheque from the bank.

- Clear N Sidwell & Sons' account.

- Record the expenditure on purchases A/c 5000.

- Update the vat account.

How Do We Do It?

We have two choices as to how we record these transactions.

- We could simply process the transaction as a bank payment, leaving no record on Sidwell's account, or

- We could create an entry in Sidwell's account for the amount and then pay that amount off. We will process the transaction this way, because it records how much we buy from each supplier.

Opening Sidwell's Account

Before we can record the transaction on Sidwell's account, we need to open a new account for N Sidwell & Sons, Old Buildings, Exeter Street, Portsmouth, PO3 2NF. Look back to the method used for Smith's Printers, follow the example and create a new account for Sidwell.

Posting the Entries

This transaction is very similar to the previous one, so we won't go into too much detail. Look back at what happened to Smith's Printers transactions for guidance. In broad terms:

- Enter Sidwell's invoice using the 'Invoices' option within 'Suppliers'

- Pay off the invoice the 'Supplier' option within 'Bank'

- Check the Bank account, Sidwells account, VAT account and Purchases account

Double Entry Transactions

Bank Current A/c 1200

		Dr	Cr
1 Jan	Personal A/c	350.00	
8 Jan	Petty Cash		50.00
8 Jan	Smiths Print		44.65
9 Jan	Sidwells		99.88

Sidwell & Sons SIDWELL

		Dr	Cr
9 Jan	Stock		99.88
9 Jan	Bank	99.88	

VAT A/c 2200/1

		Dr	Cr
8 Jan	L/heads	6.65	
9 Jan	Stock	14.88	

Purchases A/c 5000

		Dr	Cr
9 Jan	Stock	85.00	

144

12 January   Receive an order from J Roell & Co. They pay £117.50 by cash.

What Are We Trying to Do?

- Record the cash receipt of £117.50 for stock.

How Do We Do It?

The default set of accounts has account code 1230 assigned to Petty Cash. However, the software as supplied does not have an account for cash receipts from trading. For the purpose of this exercise we will create a new cash account (A/c 1225).

For the purpose of demonstration, we will process this transaction as a cash receipt. We will not process it through a customer account. This is simpler to enter but does not keep track of sales statistics by customers.

How to Create a Cash Record Account

From the main menu, select 'Bank'.

From the bank menu, select 'New'. After reading the opening screen select 'Next' which will present you with the following screen.

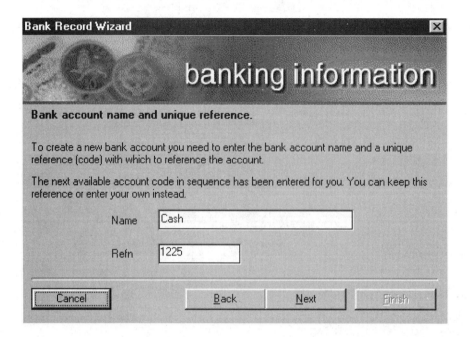

Complete the screen as shown. Press 'Next' whereupon you will be presented with the following screen. Use the drop down menu to adjust the account type to 'Cash Account'.

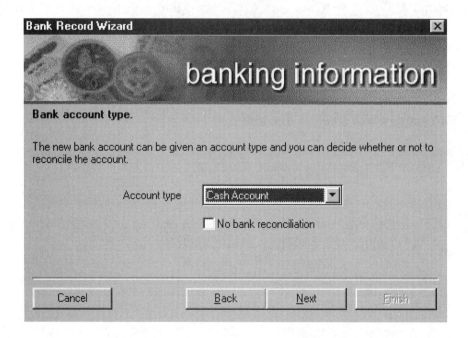

Press 'Next' to reveal the bank account details screen as below.

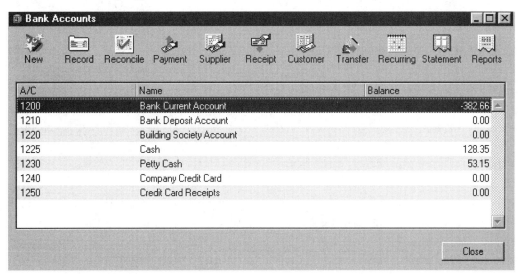

Neither this or any of the following screens are relevant so press 'Next' twice to get to the end of the Wizard, then press 'Finish'. This will return you to the bank accounts screen as shown below.

Record a Cash Receipt

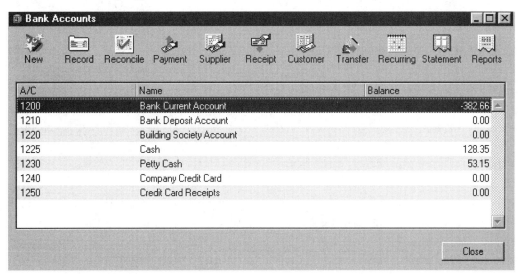

Receipt

Highlight the Cash line (A/c 1225) and select 'Receipt'. This will present you with the following screen.

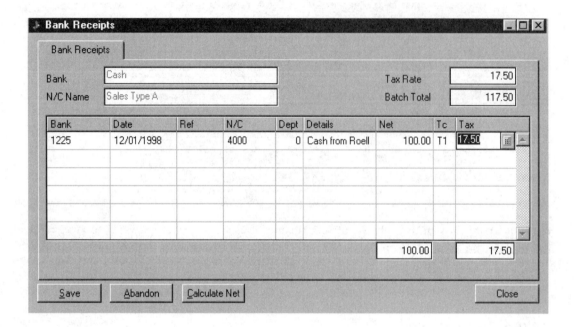

In the Bank column, select Account 1225 using the icon.

In the Date column, select 12 January 1998 with the icon.

In the Nominal Code column select 'Sales Type A', which is Nominal Code 4000.

In the Details column, enter 'cash from Roell'.

In the net column enter £117.50 then press the 'Calculate Net' button to extract the VAT amount and present the true net receipts of £100 in the net column.

Save the transactions and close all screens to return to the main menu.

Did It Work?

Check Cash Account

From the main screen, select 'Bank'. Highlight 'Cash' (A/c 1225.)

From the Bank Accounts menu select 'Record'. From within record, select 'Activity'. Note the debit entry for £117.50 shown as cash received. Close all screens to return to the main menu.

Check Sales Account

From the main menu, select 'Nominal Ledger'. Highlight the 'Sales Account Type A (A/c 4000)'. Select 'Activity', 'OK' the sub menu defaults. Note the entry of £100 of sales. Close all menus to return to the main menu.

Check VAT Account

From the main menu, select 'Nominal Account'. Highlight 'A/c 2200 Sales Tax Control Account'.

Select 'Activity'. Accept the sub menu defaults. Note the addition of £17.50 to the sales tax total. Close all menus to return to the main menu.

Double Entry Transactions

Bank Current A/c 1200				Cash A/c 1225		
	Dr	**Cr**			**Dr**	**Cr**
1 Jan Personal A/c	350.00		12 Jan Roell		117.50	
8 Jan Petty Cash		50.00				
8 Jan Smith's Print		44.65				
9 Jan Sidwell's		99.88				

VAT A/c 2200/1				Sales A/c Type A 4000		
	Dr	**Cr**			**Dr**	**Cr**
8 Jan L/heads	6.65		12 Jan Roell			100.00
9 Jan Sidwell's	14.88					
12 Jan Roell		17.50				

12 January You do work for a client who pays you £47 in cash. There are no costs other than your own time.

What Are We Trying to Do?

- Record the cash receipt of £47.00 for labour.

How Do We Do It?

From the main menu select 'Bank'. From the bank accounts menu highlight the cash account A/c 1225.

From the Bank Accounts menu, select 'Receipts'. Complete the Bank Receipts screen as shown below. Because the nature of this sale which is different to selling materials, we have coded it code 4001 Sales Type B. Note that the sale must still carry VAT even though it is cash! Save the screen and press 'Close'. Return to the main menu.

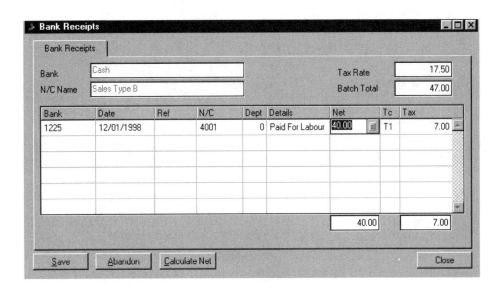

Did It Work?

Check The Sales Account

- From the main menu, select 'Nominal Ledger'.

- On the Nominal Ledger menu highlight 'A/c code 4001 Sales Type B', select 'Activity', accept the defaults.

- Note the new entry on code 4001 for £40.00 of sales turnover.

Check the VAT

- Return to the Nominal Ledger menu.

- Highlight Nominal Code 2200 'Sales Tax Control Account'.

- Select 'Activity' and accept the sub menu default.

- Note the addition of £7.00 VAT onto the account.

- Close all screens.

Check the Cash Receipts

- From the main menu, select 'Bank'.

- From the Bank Accounts menu, highlight the 'Cash' Account (A/c No. 1225)'.

- Select 'Record' and press the 'Activity' tab.

- Note the addition of £47 cash as the most recent transaction.

- Close all screens and return to the main menu.

Double Entry Transactions

	Bank Current A/c 1200			Cash A/c 1225	
	Dr	Cr		Dr	Cr
1 Jan Personal A/c	350.00		12 Jan Roell	117.50	
8 Jan Petty Cash		50.00	12 Jan Client	47.00	
8 Jan Smith's Print		44.65			
9 Jan Sidwell's		99.88			

	VAT A/c 2200/1			Sales A/c Type B 4001	
	Dr	Cr		Dr	Cr
8 Jan L/heads	6.65		12 Jan Client		40.00
9 Jan Sidwell's	14.88				
12 Jan Roell		17.50			
12 Jan Client		7.00			

14 January British Telecom demand a deposit of £117.50 before they will connect your business telephone. You pay by business cheque.

What Are We Trying to Do?

- Record the deposit for the telephone connection. (A/c 7502)

- Record the payment of £117.50 from the bank account. (A/c 1200)

How Do We Do It?

From the main menu select 'Bank'. Highlight the 'Bank Current Account'. (A/c 1200)

From the bank account menu, select 'Payment'. You will be presented with the following screen. Complete the screen as follows. The telephone account is A/c no 7502. Don't forget to use the 'Calculate Net' button to work out the vat. Save and close down all screens.

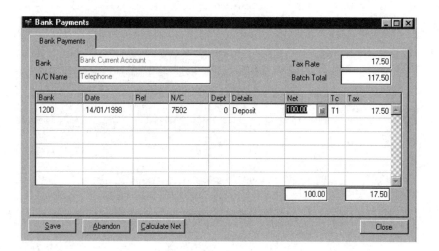

Did It Work?

Check Telephone Account (A/c No 7502)

From the main menu, select 'Nominal'. Highlight the 'Telephone' A/c No 7502.

Select 'Activity', accept the defaults on the sub menu by pressing 'OK'.

Note that the balance on the telephone account is £100 which is the payment of £117.50 less the value added tax.

Close all open screens and return to the main menu.

Check the VAT Account (A/c No 2200/1)

Select 'Nominal' from the main menu. Highlight the Purchase Tax Control A/c No 2201.

Select 'Activity' from the Nominal Ledger menu. Accept the sub menu defaults. Notice that an extra £17.50 has been added to this account. Close all screens.

Check the Bank Account (A/c No 1200)

From the main menu, select 'Bank'. Highlight the Bank Current Account A/c No 1200.

Select 'Record' from the Bank Record screen, select 'Activity'. Note the £117.50 payment as deposit.

Close all screens.

Double Entry Transactions

Bank Current A/c
1200

		Dr	Cr
1 Jan	Personal A/c	350.00	
8 Jan	Petty Cash		50.00
8 Jan	Smith's Print		44.65
9 Jan	Sidwell's		99.88
14 Jan	Brit Telecom		117.50

Cash A/c
1225

		Dr	Cr
12 Jan		Roell	117.50
12 Jan		Client	47.00

VAT A/c
2200/1

		Dr	Cr
8 Jan	L/heads	6.65	
9 Jan	Sidwells	14.88	
12 Jan	Roell		17.50
12 Jan	Client		7.00
14 Jan	Telephone	17.50	

Telephone A/c
7502

		Dr	Cr
14 Jan	Brit Tel	100.00	

14 January Ted receives a rate rebate of £28 on his house. Suspecting that the business account may be getting a little low, he pays this directly into the business account.

What Are We Trying to Do?

- Record the payment of £28 into the business capital account.

How Do We Do It?

From the main menu, select 'Bank'. Highlight the 'Bank Current Account (A/c No 1200)'.

From the Bank Accounts menu, select 'Receipts'. You will be presented with the following screen. Complete the screen as shown.

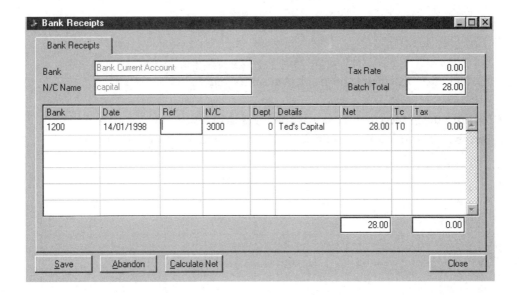

Bank	Date	Ref	N/C	Dept	Details	Net	Tc	Tax
1200	14/01/1998		3000	0	Ted's Capital	28.00	T0	0.00

Bank: Bank Current Account
N/C Name: capital
Tax Rate: 0.00
Batch Total: 28.00

28.00   0.00

Save   Abandon   Calculate Net   Close

Use the drop down menus from 'Bank', 'Date' and 'Nominal code' to make the receipts entries easier.

Save the screen and close all open menus to take you back to the main menu.

Did It Work?

Check Capital Account

- From the main menu, select 'Nominal'. From the lists of nominal codes, select 'Capital A/c 3000'.

- Select 'Activity' from the Nominal Ledger menu. Accept the sub menu defaults. Notice that an extra £28.00 of capital has been added to this account.

- Close all screens and return to the main menu.

Check Bank Balance

- From the main menu select 'Bank'. Highlight the bank 'Current Account (A/c No 1200)'.

- Select 'Record' from the Bank Accounts menu.

- From within the Bank Records screen, select 'Activity'. Note that the last entry on the current bank account is Ted's capital £28. Close all screens.

Double Entry Transactions

Bank Current A/c
1200

		Dr	Cr
1 Jan	Personal A/c	350.00	
8 Jan	Petty Cash		50.00
8 Jan	Smith's Print		44.65
9 Jan	Sidwell's		99.88
14 Jan	Brit Telecom		117.50
14 Jan	Capital introduced	28.00	

Cash A/c
1225

		Dr	Cr
12 Jan	Roell	117.50	
12 Jan	Client	47.00	

VAT A/c
2200/1

		Dr	Cr
8 Jan	L/heads	6.65	
9 Jan	Sidwell's	14.88	
12 Jan	Roell		17.50
12 Jan	Client		7.00
14 Jan	Telephone	17.50	

Capital A/c
3000

		Dr	Cr
1 Jan	Bank A/c		350.00
14 Jan	Rate Rebate		28.00

14 January You remember it is your wife's birthday after the bank has closed. Take £15 from cash (A/c 1225) to buy her a present – you keep the change for yourself.

What Are We Trying to Do?

- Record the withdrawal of £15 from Cash (A/c No 1225). Charge to Drawings (A/c 3300)

How Do We Do It?

Bank

From main menu select 'Bank'. Highlight the 'Cash Account' (A/c No 1225).

From the Bank Accounts menu select 'Payment'. You will be presented with the following screen. Complete the screen as shown.

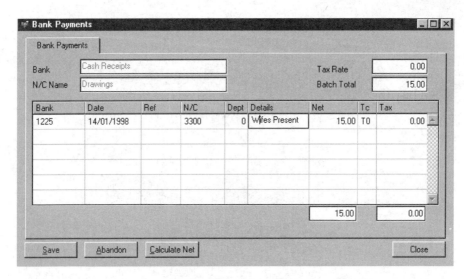

Bank	Cash Receipts					Tax Rate		0.00
N/C Name	Drawings					Batch Total		15.00

Bank	Date	Ref	N/C	Dept	Details	Net	Tc	Tax
1225	14/01/1998		3300	0	Wifes Present	15.00	T0	0.00
							15.00	0.00

Save Abandon Calculate Net Close

In this transaction we are taking £15 from the cash account (A/c no 1225). Use the drop down menu for 'Bank', 'Date' and 'Nominal account' to save data entry effort. VAT does not apply to capital transactions. Save and close the bank payments screens.

Did It Work?

Check the Drawings Account (A/c 3300)

From the main menu, select 'Nominal'. Highlight A/c No 3300 which is the Drawings account.

From the Nominal Ledger menu select 'Activity'. Accept the sub menu defaults. Note that the Drawings account has one withdrawal for the wife's present. Close all screens to return to the main menu.

Check the Cash Account A/c 1225

From the main menu, select 'Bank'. In the Bank Accounts list, highlight the 'Cash Account' (No 1225).

From the Bank Accounts menu, select 'Record'. From the Record menu, select 'Activity'. Notice that the last transaction is the withdrawal of £15 to buy the wife's present. Close all screens to return to the main menu.

Double Entry Transactions

	Bank Current A/c 1200			Cash A/c 1225	
	Dr	Cr		Dr	Cr
1 Jan Personal A/c	350.00		12 Jan Roell 117.50		
8 Jan Petty Cash		50.00	12 Jan Client 47.00		
8 Jan Smith's Print		44.65	14 Jan to Drawings		15.00
9 Jan Sidwell's		99.88			
14 Jan Brit Telecom		117.50			
14 Jan Rate Rebate	28.00				

	VAT A/c 2200/1			Drawings A/c 3300	
	Dr	Cr		Dr	Cr
8 Jan L/heads	6.65		14 Jan 98 from Cash 15.00		
9 Jan Sidwell's	14.88				
12 Jan Roell		17.50			
12 Jan Client		7.00			
14 Jan Telephone	17.50				

16 January Pay wife her wages of £25 for work in the business. You pay her by cheque.

What Are We Trying to Do?

- Record the wages payment of £25 from the bank account.

How Do We Do It?

Bank

From the main menu select 'Bank'. Highlight the Current Account (A/c No 1200).

Payment

From the Bank Accounts menu select 'Payment'. You will be presented with the following screen. Complete the screen as shown.

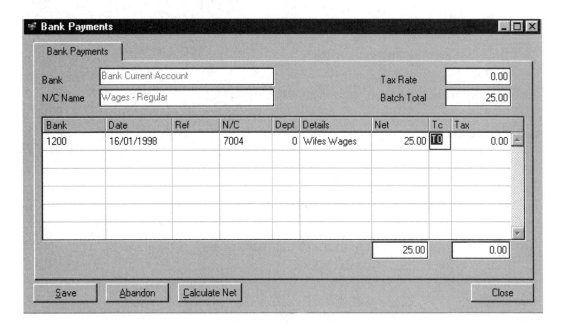

Bank	Date	Ref	N/C	Dept	Details	Net	Tc	Tax
1200	16/01/1998		7004	0	Wifes Wages	25.00	T0	0.00

Bank: Bank Current Account
N/C Name: Wages - Regular
Tax Rate: 0.00
Batch Total: 25.00

Totals: 25.00 | 0.00

Save Abandon Calculate Net Close

- Wages are recorded in Account no 7004. (wages – regular). Use VAT tax code T0 to process the transaction.

- Save the transaction and close all screens as you return to the main menu.

Did It Work?

Check Wages Account

- From the main menu select 'Nominal Ledger'.

- From the lists of accounts available, highlight Account no 7004.

- Select 'Activity' from the Nominal Ledger menu, accept the sub menu defaults.

- Note the entry for wife's wages. Close the screen and return to the main menu.

Check the Bank Account

- From the main menu select 'Bank'.

- Highlight the 'Current Bank Account (A/c 1200)'.

- Select 'Record'.

- From within Bank Record select 'Activity'.

- Notice that the last entry is for payment of wife's wages.

- Close each screen as you return to the main menu.

Double Entry Transactions

Bank Current A/c 1200				Cash A/c 1225		
	Dr	**Cr**			**Dr**	**Cr**
1 Jan Personal A/c	350.00		12 Jan Roell		117.50	
8 Jan Petty Cash		50.00	12 Jan Client		47.00	
8 Jan Smith's Print		44.65	14 Jan Drawings			15.00
9 Jan Sidwell's		99.88				
14 Jan Brit Telecom		117.50				
14 Jan Rate Rebate	28.00					
16 Jan Wages		25.00				

VAT A/c 2200/1				Wages A/c 7004		
	Dr	**Cr**			**Dr**	**Cr**
8 Jan L/heads	6.65		16 Jan Wife		25.00	
9 Jan Sidwell's	14.88					
12 Jan Roell		17.50				
12 Jan Client		7.00				
14 Jan Telephone	17.50					

18 January   You buy a printer for use in the business from Office Equipment Ltd. You pay £223.25 by business cheque.

What Are We Trying to Do?

- Record the invoice on Office Equipment Ltd's account.

- Record the receipt of the printer.

- Record the payment of £223.25 by cheque from the bank.

- Clear Office Equipment's account.

- Update the VAT account.

How Do We Do It?

Set up a New Supplier

First of all we need to record a new supplier, proceed as follows.

 From the main menu, select 'Supplier'.

 From the Suppliers menu, select 'New'. Complete the supplier wizard in exactly the same way as we set up accounts for Sidwell and Smith's. The new supplier we need to enter is Office Equipment Ltd, The Office Centre, 21 Lazenby Street, Portsmouth, Hants PO1 2VN. There is no opening balance to be entered for this new supplier.

Complete all screens and return to the main menu.

Record the Purchase

From the main menu, select 'Supplier's.

From the Suppliers screen, select 'Invoices'.

You will be presented with the following screen. Complete the screen as shown. Notice that we have put the printer to Account no 0030 Office Equipment.

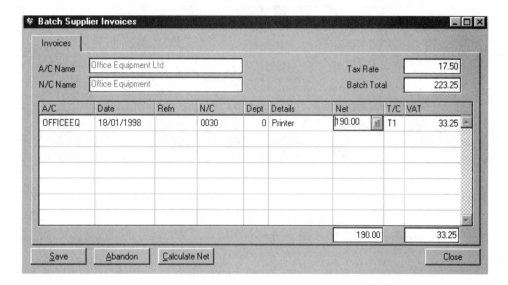

Save the data and close all screens as you return to the main menu.

Pay for Printer

From the main menu, select 'Bank'. Highlight the 'Bank Current Account (A/c 1200)'.

From the Bank Accounts menu, select 'Suppliers'.

You will be presented with the following screen. Complete the screen as shown. Use the drop down menus and the 'Pay in full' button to make data entry easier. Save and close all screens.

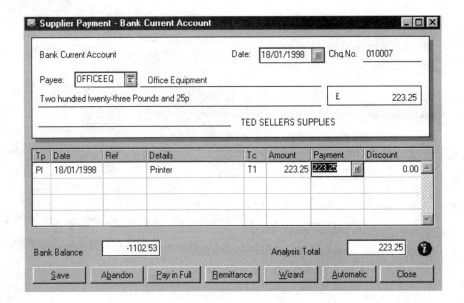

Did It Work?

Check Office Equipment Customer Account

- From the main menu, select 'Suppliers'. From the Suppliers list, highlight 'Office Equipment Ltd'.

- From the Suppliers menu select 'Activity'. Accept the defaults. Note that the Office Equipment account is cleared – the debits and credits balance each other out. Close all screens.

Check the Office Equipment Nominal Account (A/c No 0030)

- From the main menu select 'Nominal'. From the list of nominal ledger accounts highlight 'Office Equipment (0030)'.

- Select 'Activity' and accept the sub menu defaults. Notice that the office equipment account now contains an entry of £190.00 (ex VAT) for the printer.

- Close the activity screen.

- Close all screens to return to the main menu again.

Check VAT Account

- From the main menu select 'Nominal'.

- From the Nominal Ledger, highlight 'Purchase Tax Control Account' (A/c No 2201).

- From the Nominal Ledger account, select 'Activity', accept the sub menu defaults.

- Notice that the last entry is for the £33.25 VAT associated with the purchase of the printer.

- Close all menus to return to the main menu.

Check Bank Account

- From the main menu, select 'Bank'.

- From the Bank menu, highlight 'Bank current Account' (A/c No 1200).

- Select 'Record' followed by the 'Activity' tab.

- Note that the latest purchase payment shown is that of £223.25 for the printer.

Double Entry Transactions

Bank Current A/c
1200

	Dr	Cr
1 Jan Personal A/c	350.00	
8 Jan Petty Cash		50.00
8 Jan Smith's Print		44.65
9 Jan Sidwell's		99.88
14 Jan Brit Telecom		117.50
14 Jan Rate Rebate	28.00	
16 Jan Wages		25.00
18 Jan Printer		223.25

Cash A/c
1225

	Dr	Cr
12 Jan Roell	117.50	
12 Jan Client	47.00	
14 Jan Drawings		15.00

VAT A/c
2200/1

	Dr	Cr
8 Jan L/heads	6.65	
9 Jan Sidwell's	14.88	
12 Jan Roell		17.50
12 Jan Client		7.00
14 Jan Telephone	17.50	
18 Jan Printer	33.25	

Office Equipment A/c
0030

	Dr	Cr
18 Jan Printer	190.00	

Office Equipment A/c

	Dr	Cr
18 Jan Printer		223.25
18 Jan Bank	223.25	

22 January You receive an invoice from your accountant Boris Knocker for £125 plus VAT. You pay this from your business account.

What Are We Trying to Do?

- Set up a new supplier account.

- Record the invoice on the new account.

- Record the payment of £125 (plus VAT) by cheque from the bank.

- Clear Boris Knocker's account.

- Update the VAT account.

How Do We Do It?

- In this instance, we will set up a new suppliers account for the accountant. However, if you only anticipate receiving one invoice a year then you probably would not find it worthwhile to create a supplier account for a single transaction.

Open New Supplier Account

- Look back to the previous instruction for Smith's, Sidwell's and Office Equipment Ltd to see how to create a new supplier account. Create an account for Boris Knocker, 35 Perth Street, Portsmouth, Hants PO2 7TH.

Post the accountant's bill to the Suppliers Account

From the main menu select 'Supplier', highlight 'Boris Knocker'.

Select 'Invoices'.

Complete the screen as shown below. Note that accountancy fees are entered under nominal code 7601 – Accounts and Accountancy Fees. 'Save' and close the screen.

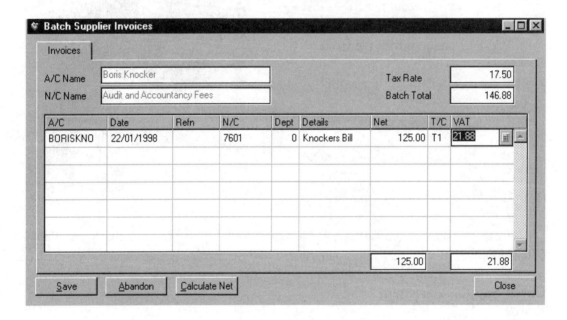

Pay Off the Invoice

From the main menu, select 'Bank'. Highlight the 'Bank Current Account' ie Account no 1200.

From the Bank Accounts menu, select 'Supplier'. Complete as follows. Use the dropdown menus to speed data entry.

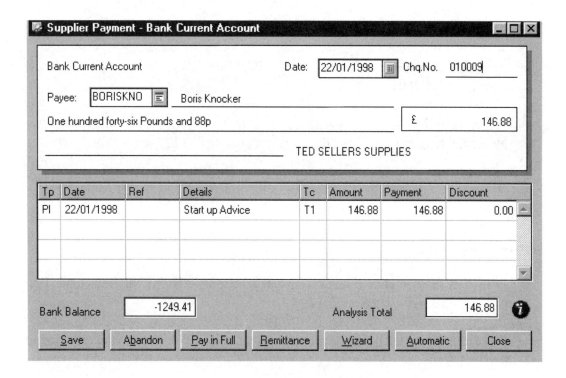

Close all screens. Return to the main menu.

Did It Work?

Check Suppliers Account

- From the main menu select the 'Suppliers' icon.

- Highlight Boris Knocker in the Suppliers menu.

- Select 'Activity', accept the sub menu defaults.

- Notice that Boris Knocker account has been cleared to a zero balance.

- Close all screens to return to the main menu.

Check the Accounts Nominal Code

- From the main menu, select 'Nominal'. Highlight 'Accounts and Accountancy Fees (A/c No 7601)'.

- Select 'Activity' from the Nominal Ledger menu, accept the sub menu defaults. Note that Account no 7601 now carries a cheque of £125 (ex VAT).

- Close all screens to return to the main menu.

Check VAT Account

- From the main menu, select 'Nominal Accounts'. Highlight 'Purchase Tax Control Account (A/c No 2201)'.

- From the Nominal Ledger Account select 'Activity', accept the sub menu defaults.

- Note that the last entry was for £21.88 which was the VAT charge on the Boris Knocker invoice.

- Close all screens to return to the main menu.

Check Bank Account Balance

- From the main menu, select 'Bank'. Highlight the 'Bank Current Account' (A/c No 1200).

- Select 'Record' followed by 'Activity' from the Bank Record menu.

- Scroll down the list, note that the last entry was the payment to Boris Knocker for £146.88.

- Close all screens to return to the main menu.

Double Entry Transactions

Bank Current A/c
1200

		Dr	Cr
1 Jan	Personal A/c	350.00	
8 Jan	Petty Cash		50.00
8 Jan	Smith's Print		44.65
9 Jan	Sidwell's		99.88
14 Jan	Brit Telecom		117.50
14 Jan	Rate Rebate	28.00	
16 Jan	Wages		25.00
18 Jan	Printer		223.25
22 Jan	Accountant		146.88

Cash A/c
1225

		Dr	Cr
12 Jan	Roell	117.50	
12 Jan	Client	47.00	
14 Jan	Drawings		15.00

VAT A/c
2200/1

		Dr	Cr
8 Jan	L/heads	6.65	
9 Jan	Sidwell's	14.88	
12 Jan	Roell		17.50
12 Jan	Client		7.00
14 Jan	Telephone	17.50	
18 Jan	Printer	33.25	
22 Jan	Accountant	21.88	

Accountancy Fees A/c
7601

		Dr	Cr
18 Jan	Knocker	125.00	

Boris Knocker

		Dr	Cr
22 Jan	Fees		146.88
22 Jan	Bank	146.88	

26 January You see some office furniture which you would like to buy from Office Equipment Ltd. You leave a cheque as deposit for £23.50 and persuade them to hold it for you pending later payment and collection.

What Are We Trying to Do?

- Record the furniture deposit paid by cheque.

How Do We Do It?

From the main menu, select 'Suppliers'. Highlight 'Office Equipment'.

From the suppliers menu, select 'Invoices'. You will be presented with the screen shown below. Complete the screen as shown. Use the Furniture and Fixtures Account (A/c 0040).

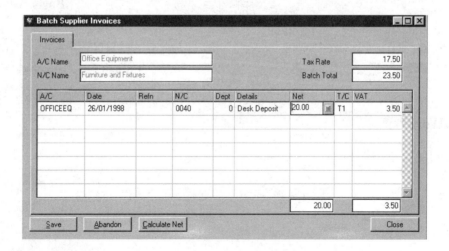

Save the data and close the screen. So far we have recorded the deposit. Now we need to pay it off. Close all open screens to return to the main menu.

From the main menu select 'Bank'. Highlight the bank current account. (A/c No 1200).

From the 'Bank Accounts' menu select 'Supplier'. Complete the screen as shown.

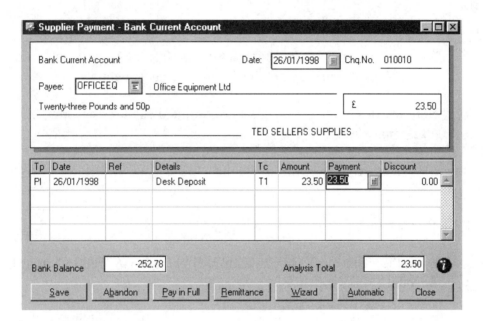

Close all screens and return to the main menu.

Did It Work?

Check Office Equipment Account

From the main menu select, 'Suppliers'. Highlight 'Office Equipment Ltd'.

From the Suppliers menu, select 'Activity', accept the sub menu range defaults.

Note that the last item in the Office Equipment account is the desk deposit.

Close all screens to return to the main menu.

Check Office Furniture Account

From the main menu select 'Nominal'.

From the nominal account list, select 'A/c 0040, Furniture and Fixtures'. Select 'Activity' and accept the transaction range defaults.

Note the desk appears on the Furniture and Fixtures account, cost £20 (excluding VAT).

Close all screens to return to the main menu.

Check Bank Account

From the main menu, select 'Bank'. Highlight 'A/c 1200 Current Bank Account'.

From the Bank Accounts menu select 'Record' followed by the 'Activity' tab.

Scroll down the list of Bank transactions noting what the last item was, a purchase payment of £23.50. Close all screens.

Check VAT Account

From the main menu select 'Nominal'. From the list of nominal account codes highlight 'Purchase Tax Control Account (No 2201).

Select 'Activity' from the Nominal Ledger. Accept the sub menu defaults. Note the appearance of £3.50 on the VAT account. Close all screens.

Double Entry Transactions

Bank Current A/c 1200

		Dr	Cr
1 Jan	Personal A/c	350.00	
8 Jan	Petty Cash		50.00
8 Jan	Smith's Print		44.65
9 Jan	Sidwell's		99.88
14 Jan	Brit Telecom		117.50
14 Jan	Rate Rebate	28.00	
16 Jan	Wages		25.00
18 Jan	Printer		223.25
22 Jan	Accountant		146.88
26 Jan	Desk		23.50

Cash A/c 1225

		Dr	Cr
12 Jan	Roell	117.50	
12 Jan	Client	47.00	
14 Jan	Drawings		15.00

VAT A/c 2200/1

		Dr	Cr
8 Jan	L/heads	6.65	
9 Jan	Sidwell's	14.88	
12 Jan	Roell		17.50
12 Jan	Client		7.00
14 Jan	Telephone	17.50	
18 Jan	Printer	33.25	
22 Jan	Accountant	21.88	
26 Jan	Desk	3.50	

Office Equipment A/c 0030

		Dr	Cr
18 Jan	Printer	190.00	

Office Furniture A/c 0040

		Dr	Cr
26 Jan	Desk	20.00	

Note 1   **During the month you sold goods on credit to Roell raising the invoices by hand. The invoices amounted to £762 plus VAT. You meant to enter the sales invoice at the time but never got round to it. Do it now.**

What Are We Tying to Do?

- Record J Roell as a new credit customer.

- Record the sales invoice on J Roell & Co's account.

How Do We Do It?

Enter New Customer

    From the Main Menu select, 'Customers'.

    From the Customer menu, select the 'New' wizard.

Follow the directions on the customer information screens to input a new customer, J Roell & Co, 10 Farlington Road, Southsea, PO6 5CV.

Give J Roell & Co a credit limit of £2000 with 30 day Settlement Due days and 30 days Payment Due days. There is no opening balance on his account.

Record Customers Inovice

From the main menu select 'Customers'. Highlight 'J Roell & Co'.

From the Customers menu select 'Invoices'. You will be presented with the following screen. Complete the screen as shown.

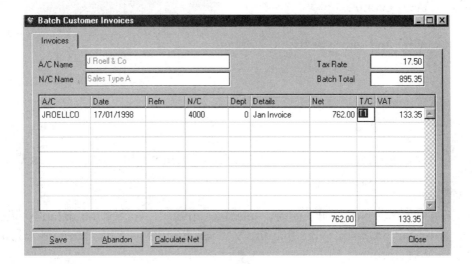

Save and close all screens and return to the main menu.

Did It Work?

Check Customers Account

From the main menu, select 'Customers'. Highlight 'J Roell & Co'.

From the Customers menu, select 'Activity'. Accept the 'Activity Date Range' defaults. Note that J Roell's account now shows the amount owed by them.

Close all screens and return to the main menu.

Check the Sales Account

From the main menu, select 'Nominal'. Highlight 'Sales Account Type A (A/c No 4000)'.

Select 'Activity' from the Nominal Ledger menu. Accept the defaults offered. Notice the credit of the value of the invoice net of VAT onto the sales account.

Close all screens and return to the main menu.

Check the VAT account

From the main menu, select 'Nominal'. Highlight the 'Sales Tax Control Account (A/c No 2200).

From the Nominal Ledger, select 'Activity'. Accept the defaults offered by the program. Note that the VAT on Roell's sale has been added to the VAT account.

Close all screens and return to the main menu.

Double Entry Transactions

Bank Current A/c
1200

		Dr	Cr
1 Jan	Personal A/c	350.00	
8 Jan	Petty Cash		50.00
8 Jan	Smith's Print		44.65
9 Jan	Sidwell's		99.88
14 Jan	Brit Telecom		117.50
14 Jan	Rate Rebate	28.00	
16 Jan	Wages		25.00
18 Jan	Printer		223.25
22 Jan	Accountant		146.88
26 Jan	Desk		23.50

Cash A/c
1225

		Dr	Cr
12 Jan	Roell	117.50	
12 Jan	Client	47.00	
14 Jan	Drawings		15.00

VAT A/c
2200/1

		Dr	Cr
8 Jan	L/heads	6.65	
9 Jan	Sidwell's	14.88	
12 Jan	Roell		17.50
12 Jan	Client		7.00
14 Jan	Telephone	17.50	
18 Jan	Printer	33.25	
22 Jan	Accountant	21.88	
26 Jan	Desk	3.50	
17 Jan	Roell		133.35

J Roell & Co A/c

		Dr	Cr
17 Jan	Stock	895.35	

Sales A/c Type A
4000

		Dr	Cr
12 Jan	Roell		100.00
17 Jan	Roell		762.00

Note 2   At the end of the month you estimate that you have in stock £15 worth of the purchases that you made.

What Are We Trying to Do?

- Record the closing stock of £15.

How Do We Do It?

 From the main menu select 'Nominal'.

 From the Nominal Ledger menu select 'Journals'. This will reveal the screen shown below.

Complete the screen as shown below (remember to change the date to 30 January 1998). Opening stock code is A/c 5200 – closing stock code is A/c 5201.

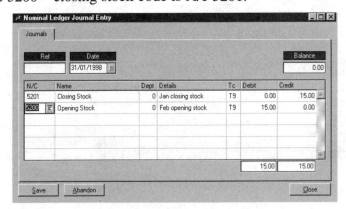

Press 'Save' and close the Nominal Ledger screens.

Did It Work?

- Check Nominal Account no's 5200 and 5201 to see if the correct entries have been posted.

Note 3   You have arranged for your National Insurance to be paid by direct debit from your business account on the 16th of every month. The cost is currently £30 per month.

What Are We Trying to Do?

- Record the NI payment of £30 from the bank account.

Note: National Insurance payments for sole traders and partnerships are personal expenses not business expenses. This is why this National Insurance payment is put to 'Drawings' A/c 3300.

From the main menu select 'Bank'. Highlight current Bank Account (A/c 1200).

From Bank Accounts select 'Payments'. You will be presented with the following screen. Complete the screen as shown.

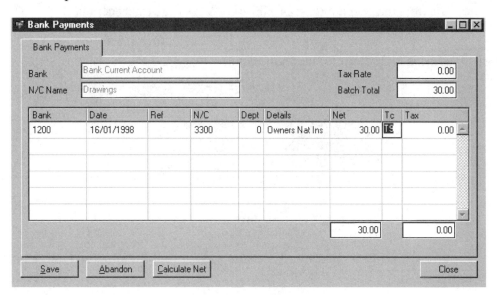

Bank	Date	Ref	N/C	Dept	Details	Net	Tc	Tax
1200	16/01/1998		3300	0	Owners Nat Ins	30.00	T9	0.00

Bank Payments

Bank — Bank Current Account
N/C Name — Drawings

Tax Rate — 0.00
Batch Total — 30.00

30.00   0.00

Save   Abandon   Calculate Net   Close

Did It Work?

Check Bank A/c

From the main menu, select 'Bank'. Highlight 'Bank Current Account (A/c 1200)'.

From Bank Accounts screen, select 'Record' followed by the 'Activity' tab. Note the payment of £30 of owner's NI.

Close all screens and return to the main menu.

Check Drawing Account 3300

From the main menu, select 'Nominal'. Highlight 'Drawings A/c no 7001'.

From the Nominal Ledger, select 'A/c no 7001'. Accept the defaults sub menu. Note the addition of £30 to owners drawings account.

Close all screens and return to the main menu.

Double Entry Transactions

Bank Current A/c 1200				Cash A/c 1225			
		Dr	**Cr**			**Dr**	**Cr**
1 Jan	Personal A/c	350.00		12 Jan	Roell	117.50	
8 Jan	Petty Cash		50.00	12 Jan	Client	47.00	
8 Jan	Smith's Print		44.65	14 Jan	Drawings		15.00
9 Jan	Sidwell's		99.88				
14 Jan	Brit Telecom		117.50				
14 Jan	Rate Rebate	28.00					
16 Jan	Wages		25.00				
18 Jan	Printer		223.25				
22 Jan	Accountant		146.88				
26 Jan	Desk		23.50				
16 Jan	DHSS – NI		30.00				

VAT A/c 2200/1				Drawings A/c 3300			
		Dr	**Cr**			**Dr**	**Cr**
8 Jan	L/heads	6.65		14 Jan	Wife's present	15.00	
9 Jan	Sidwell's	14.88		16 Jan	Nat ins	30.00	
9 Jan	Jones	87.50					
10 Jan	Roell		8.75				
12 Jan	Roell		17.50				
12 Jan	Client		7.00				
14 Jan	Telephone	17.50					
18 Jan	Printer	33.25					
22 Jan	Accountant	21.88					
26 Jan	Desk	3.50					
17 Jan	Roell		133.35				

Note 5   Petty Cash was topped up from cash by £21.15 on 30 January. The only receipt in the petty cash was a refreshments bill of £18 total. No subsequent petty cash payments were made after this date. Record the transaction for cash, A/c 1225, petty cash, A/c 1230 and subsistence (A/c 7406).

What Are We Trying to Do?

• Record the Petty Cash top up from cash account.

How Do We Do It?

Top up Petty Cash

   From the main menu, select 'Bank Accounts'.

   From Bank Accounts, select the 'Transfer' icon. You will be presented with the following screen. Complete the screen as shown. Save the data.

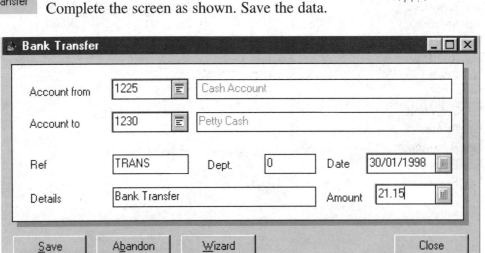

Close all screens and return to the main menu.

Record Where Petty Cash Went to

Bank

From the main menu, select 'Bank Accounts'. Highlight 'Petty Cash' followed by 'Payments'. You will be presented with the following screen. Complete the screen as shown.

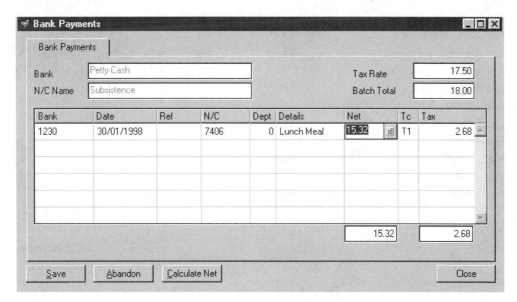

Save the entry, close all screens and return to the main menu.

Did It Work?

Record Payment of Petty Cash as Refreshments

Nominal

From the main menu select 'Nominal'. Highlight the 'Subsistence' Account (A/c 7406)'.

Activity

Select 'Activity'. Accept the defaults sub menu by pressing 'OK'. Note the entry for lunch.

Close all open screens. Check that the cash and petty cash accounts show the correct entries.

Double Entry Transactions

Bank Current A/c 1200

		Dr	Cr
1 Jan	Personal A/c	350.00	
8 Jan	Petty Cash		50.00
8 Jan	Smith's Print		44.65
9 Jan	Sidwell's		99.88
14 Jan	Brit Telecom		117.50
14 Jan	Rate Rebate	28.00	
16 Jan	Wages		25.00
18 Jan	Printer		223.25
22 Jan	Accountant		146.88
26 Jan	Desk		23.50
16 Jan	DHSS – NI		30.00

Cash A/c 1225

		Dr	Cr
12 Jan	Roell	117.50	
12 Jan	Client	47.00	
14 Jan	Drawings		15.00
30 Jan	P/Cash		21.15

VAT A/c 2200/1

		Dr	Cr
8 Jan	L/heads	6.65	
9 Jan	Sidwell's	14.88	
12 Jan	Roell		17.50
12 Jan	Client		7.00
14 Jan	Telephone	17.50	
18 Jan	Printer	33.25	
22 Jan	Accountant	21.88	
26 Jan	Desk	3.50	
31 Jan	Roell		133.35
30 Jan	P/Cash	2.68	

Subsistence A/c 7406

		Dr	Cr
30 Jan	Lunch	15.32	

Petty Cash A/c 1230

		Dr	Cr
8 Jan	from Bank	50.00	
30 Jan	from Cash	21.15	
30 Jan	Lunch		18.00

Note 6   You estimate that you have used £20 worth of electricity during the month.

What Are We Trying to Do?

- Record an accrual of £20 for electricity.

How Do We Do It?

From the main menu, select 'Nominal'.

From the Nominal Ledger menu, select 'Journals'. This will reveal the Nominal Ledger Journal entry screen shown below.

Complete the screen as shown, remember to change the date to 30 January 1998. Electricity is A/c no 7200, Accruals is A/c no 2109.

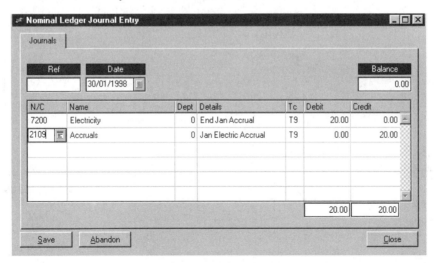

Press 'Save' and close the Nominal Ledger Journal entry screen.

Did It Work?

Check Electricity Account no 7200 and Accruals Account no 2109.

Double Entry Transactions

Bank Current A/c 1200	Dr	Cr		Cash A/c 1225	Dr	Cr
1 Jan Personal A/c	350.00		12 Jan Roell		117.50	
8 Jan Petty Cash		50.00	12 Jan Client		47.00	
8 Jan Smith's Print		44.65	14 Jan Drawings			15.00
9 Jan Sidwell's		99.88	30 Jan P/Cash			21.15
14 Jan Brit Telecom		117.50				
14 Jan Rate Rebate	28.00					
16 Jan Wages		25.00				
18 Jan Printer		223.25				
22 Jan Accountant		146.88				
26 Jan Desk		23.50				
16 Jan DHSS – NI		30.00				

VAT A/c 2200/1	Dr	Cr		Electricity A/c 7200	Dr	Cr
8 Jan L/heads	6.65		31 Jan Est	20.00	
9 Jan Sidwell's	14.88				
12 Jan Roell		17.50			
12 Jan Client		7.00			
14 Jan Telephone	17.50				
18 Jan Printer	33.25				
22 Jan Accountant	21.88				
26 Jan Desk	3.50				
17 Jan Roell		133.35			
30 Jan P/Cash	3.15				

Accruals A/c 2109	Dr	Cr
31 Jan Elec		20.00

How to Print a Set of Accounts

To Print the Profit and Loss Account

Financials

From the main menu select 'Financials'. Highlight 'Profit and Loss Account'. You will be offered selection criteria for dates. Adjust to read as follows.

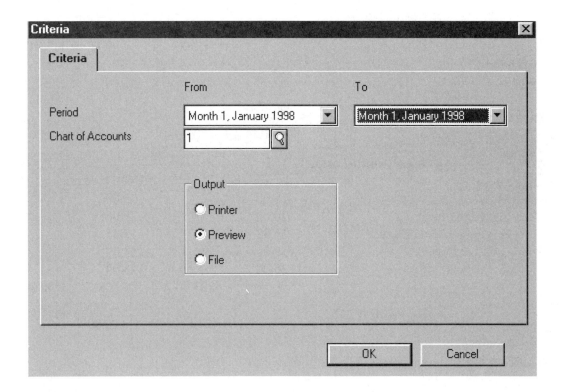

If you 'OK' the criteria screen, you will be presented with a screen showing a small part of the profit and loss account. Select 'Print' from the base of this window to print the profit and loss account.

Close the Profit and Loss A/c window to return to the Financials screen.

Date: 28/10/1998   **TED SELLERS SUPPLIES**   **Page:** 1
Time: 23:32:55   **Profit & Loss**

From: Month 1, January 1998
To: Month 1, January 1998

Chart of Accounts: Default Chart of Accounts

	Period		**Year to Date**	
Sales				
Product Sales	902.00		902.00	
		902.00		902.00
Purchases				
Purchases	85.00		85.00	
		85.00		85.00
Direct Expenses				
		0.00		0.00
Gross Profit/(Loss):		817.00		817.00
Overheads				
Gross Wages	25.00		25.00	
Heat, Light and Power	20.00		20.00	
Travelling and Entertainment	15.32		15.32	
Printing and Stationery	138.00		138.00	
Professional Fees	125.00		125.00	
		323.00		323.32
Net Profit/(Loss):		493.68		493.68

To Print the Balance Sheet

Financials

From the main menu, select 'Financials'. From the Financials menu, select 'Balance'.

Adjust the criteria screen to show the same dates as that shown previously for the profit and loss account. Press 'OK' to preview the screen. If want to print from the screen press printout the small part of the balance sheet visible.

Date: 28/10/1998   **TED SELLERS SUPPLIES**   **Page:** 1
Time: 23:37:41   **Balance Sheet**

From: Month 1, January 1998
To: Month 1, January 1998

Chart of Account: Default Chart of Accounts

	Period		Year to Date	
Fixed Assets				
Office Equipment	190.00		190.00	
Furniture and Fixtures	20.00		20.00	
		210.00		210.00
Current Assets				
Debtors	895.35		895.35	
Deposits and Cash	181.50		181.50	
		1,076.85		1,076.85
Current Liabilities				
Creditors: Short Term	20.00		20.00	
Bank Account	382.66		382.66	
VAT Liability	57.51		57.51	
		460.17		460.17
Current Assets less Liabilities:		616.68		616.68
Net Assets:		826.68		826.68
Capital & Reserves				
Share Capital	378.00		378.00	
Drawings	(45.00)		(45.00)	
P&L Account	493.68		493.68	
		826.68		826.68

Answer to Double Entry Exercise on Page 107

Bank

		Dr	Cr
12 May	Cash Sale	94.00	
16 May	Cash Sale	70.50	
26 May	Smith	564.00	

Sales

		Dr	Cr
12 May	Cash Sale		80.00
16 May	Cash Sale		60.00
20 May	Credit Sale		600.00
21 May	Smith Refund	120.00	
29 May	Credit Sale		300.00

Smith

		Dr	Cr
20 May	Goods	705.00	
21 May	Refund		141.00
26 May	Bal of Sale		564.00

Evans

		Dr	Cr
29 May	Goods	352.50	

VAT

		Dr	Cr
12 May	Cash Sale		14.00
16 May	Cash Sale		10.50
20 May	Credit sale		105.00
21 May	Smith Rfd	21.00	
29 May	Credit Sale		52.50

Glossary of Accounting Terms

Account
A personal or impersonal record of one or more business transactions to enable a balance to be taken at any moment in time.

Accountancy
The process of analysing, classifying and recording transactions and operations in terms of time, quantity and money.

Accounting Period
The period for which financial accounts are customarily prepared.

Accounting System
The day-to-day method by which transactions are recorded and, ultimately, appear in the financial accounts.

Accrual Accounting
Recognition of revenues and costs in the accounts for the period in which they were earned or incurred rather than the period in which the cash is actually received or disbursed.

Advice Note
See 'Delivery Note'.

Aged Analysis
Usually used on a schedule of sales ledger balances to indicate the age of the balances (eg one month old, two months old, over six months etc).

Asset
Goods, resources and property of all kinds belonging to a company, or to an individual, which are used in the business.

Balance Sheet	A statement showing the assets and liabilities of any trading concern, at any particular moment in time.
Balancing the Books	The periodical closing off and adjusting of all accounts in the ledger, in order to ascertain the profit or loss made during a period.
Bank Reconciliation	A statement explaining the difference between the balance of an account reported by a bank and the account appearing in the books of the bank's client (see 'Reconciliation Statement').
Book-keeping	The technique of keeping accounts – of recording in a regular, concise and accurate manner the business transactions of an entity in a set of books kept for the purpose.
Books of Account	A set of books which records the business transactions of a firm or company etc (see 'Book-keeping').
Capital	The finance supplied by the proprietors of a business in order to acquire the resources (assets) with which to operate.
Cash Book	A book in which an account (record) is kept of all receipts and payments of money, by cash or cheque.
Cash Received Abstract	A form showing the cash received from all sources for each working day of the week.
Close Off	To transfer to the profit and loss account in the nominal ledger, from each account concerned, the amount itemised in the published profit and loss account so as to leave, as balances, only those which are included on the balance sheet.
Contra	The matching of debits with credits or the setting off of one against the other (also known as 'netting off').

Control Account   A memorandum account consisting of totals of all items debited or credited to a number of individual accounts in a ledger so that the total account may represent the individual accounts when drafting financial statements. Frequently used for sales and purchases ledgers and may be utilised to provide a means of control where one clerk writes up the individual accounts in a ledger and another independently maintains a control account for that ledger (also known as a 'total account').

Credit   An entry on the right hand side of a ledger account. To 'credit' an account is to make an entry on the right hand side.

Credit Note   Document sent to a person, firm, etc stating that their account is credited with the amount stated (eg when goods are returned by that person, firm etc or an allowance is made to that person, firm etc).

Creditor   One to whom money is owed for goods, cash, services etc.

Creditors Ledger   A book of account which records the personal side of all credit supplies of goods or services (also known as the 'bought ledger').

Current Assets   That group of assets in a cash or near cash state (eg cash, debtors, stock).

Debit   An entry on the left hand side of a ledger account. To 'debit' an account is to make an entry on the left hand side.

Debit Note   Document sent to a person, company etc stating that their account is debited with the amount stated (eg as for credit note when goods are returned due to some imperfection or to correct an overcharge).

Debtor   One who owes money for goods, cash, services supplied.

Debtors Ledger A book of account which records the personal side of all sales, on credit, of goods or services (also known as the 'Sales Ledger').

Delivery Note Note accompanying the delivery of goods or services ordered (sometimes known as the despatch or advice note).

Depreciation The measure of the estimated loss in money value of a fixed asset owing to use, obsolescence or passage of time.

Despatch Note *See* 'Delivery Note'.

Discount An allowance deducted from an invoice price, account etc.

Double-entry Method of book-keeping in which two entries are made for each transaction in order to record the two aspects which every transaction has and to provide a means of proving the entries by balancing the ledgers in which each transaction is recorded.

Entry The record of a transaction in a book of account.

Extended Trial Balance An extension of the 'trial balance' to facilitate adjustments and closing entries for the purpose of preparing financial statements, and to allocate each balance to the profit and loss account or the balance sheet or to supporting summaries thereto (also known as 'Analysed Trial Balance').

Final Accounts The profit and loss account, balance sheet and associated notes as agreed by the proprietor of the business.

Fixed Asset An asset which is in permanent use within a business, eg land, buildings, furniture, plant, machinery etc.

Goodwill 'Benefits arising from connection and reputation'. In the case of an established trade or business, it is the connection and advantages accruing to it. The goodwill of a business is frequently a most valuable asset but is not capable of accurate measurement.

Gross	A total without any deductions.
Grossing Up	The calculation of a gross figure from a net figure by adding back the deductions.
Imprest System	Method by which a fixed amount is advanced, and the expenditure from the amount at the end of the month or period reimbursed, so that the monthly or periodic balance remains the same (frequently used for petty cash floats).
Intangible Asset	Asset which is neither fixed nor current yet possesses value (eg goodwill).
Inventory	The stock-in-trade and work in progress of a business at any given time.
Invoice	A document showing the character, quantity, price, terms, nature of delivery and other particulars of goods sold or services rendered.
Journal	Literally, the book containing an account of each day's transactions. Now used for the entry of those transactions which cannot be entered in the bought or sales day books or cash books.
Ledger	A collection of accounts. The principal book of account in which the entries from all the other books are summarised, divided into cash book, bought ledger, sales ledger and nominal ledger.
Liabilities	A term denoting the combined debts owed by a firm, company etc.
Liquidity	The excess of cash or near cash assets over current liabilities.
Net	The amount of any charge or cost after all deductions have been made.
Nominal Accounts	Accounts for the income and expenses of a business.

Nominal Ledger   Otherwise known as the impersonal or general ledger. The ledger which contains impersonal accounts.

Personal Account   An account showing transactions with a particular person, firm or company, as distinct from a nominal account.

Petty Cash Book   A book subsidiary to the cash book in which are recorded all small cash payments.

Posting   The transfer of entries from the books of prime entry to their separate accounts in the ledgers.

Prepayment   A payment made in the accounting period of which part or all relates to a future period.

Profit & Loss Account   A summary of all revenue accounts showing, as its balance, the profit (or loss) for the accounting period.

Provisions   Amounts written off or retained out of profits to provide for depreciation, renewals or diminution in value of assets, or retained to provide for any known liability of which the amount cannot be determined with accuracy.

Purchase   Any expense for goods or services supplied to the business.

Purchases Day Book   A book of prime entry used to list, analyse and summarise all purchases and services supplied on credit (also known as the 'Bought Day Book').

Reconciliation   A statement showing the process whereby the balances of two accounts, independently written up in respect of the same transactions, which, shown an apparent discrepancy, are brought into agreement. The most common reconciliation statement is that used to bring into agreement the cash book and bank statement balances (see 'Bank Reconciliation').

Reserves   Profits retained within the business.

Returns	Goods returned to the supplier because they are faulty, damaged or not what was ordered.
Revenue	Income received from any source.
Sales Day Book	A book of prime entry used to list, analyse and summarise all the invoices for credit sales transactions.
Sales Ledger	See 'Debtors Ledger'.
Statement (of account)	An account, periodically rendered, showing the amounts due by one person or firm to another. Generally, a statement contains only the dates and amounts of each invoice sent since the previous settlement.
Statutory Accounts	Accounts prepared in a form suitable for submission to the Registrar of Companies for filing.
Stock (-in-trade)	Goods held for sale in the ordinary course of business.
Suspense Account	A temporary account for a posting which requires further investigation (eg unexplained items in the bank statement).
Tangible Asset	An asset which is either fixed or current.
Total Account	See 'Control Account'.
Transfer	An amount taken from one account and restated in another.
Trial Balance	A summary listing of all the balances in the ledgers of a business to prove the arithmetical accuracy and the completion of the double entry.
Turnover	Net sales, ie total sales less allowances.
Vouching	The process of checking information in books of account to the original documentation.

Index

Through Kogan Page all readers can enjoy the benefits of Call Sciences' *Personal Assistant*®
- the complete Call Management System

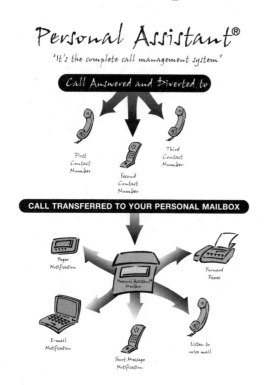

CALL ME – Your clients, friends and family only need ONE NUMBER to contact you rather than separate numbers for mobile, home, office and fax.

FAX ME – You choose where and when your faxes are delivered to any fax machine – you control whether your faxes are forwarded straight away or stored until you collect them.

FIND ME – *Personal Asistant*® searches you at up to 3 locations according to your typical weekly availability schedule – and it even remembers where it last found you.

When you are not available, your calls are automatically routed to voice mail. Whenever a message is received, you are notified by pager, GSM short message or e-mail.

Why have a *Personal Assistant*® number?

- Your own receptionist 24 hours a day
- Your personal number is never engaged
- Greets your callers in a professional manner
- Holds your contact numbers and knows where to find you
- Tells you who is calling before putting them through
- Transfers to another number or voice mail part way through a call
- Knows when you do not normally wish to be disturbed
- Takes voice and fax messages when you are not available
- Faxes delivered to any fax machine
- Charge card option for outgoing calls

All for less than 25p per day

Call Sciences™

QMS ✓
ISO 9002
REGISTERED FIRM

Call 0800 689 9999 today to activate your Personal Assistant®!